Stitched Together

Fresh Projects and Ideas for Group Quilting

BY JILL FINLEY OF JILLILY STUDIO

KANSAS CITY STAR QUILTS
Continuing the Tradition

Stitched Together
Fresh Projects and Ideas for Group Quilting

By: Jill Finley of Jillily Studio
Editor: Kent Richards
Technical Editor: Nan Doljac
Book Design: Amy Robertson

Photography: Aaron T. Leimkuehler
Illustration: Lon Eric Craven
Production Assistance: Jo Ann Groves

Jillily Studio Needle Arts
Visit Jill's website at jillilystudio.com for more Jillily Studio designs and products.

Props for photos from Dear Lizzie in Highland, Utah.
mydearlizzie.com

Published by:
Kansas City Star Books
1729 Grand Blvd.
Kansas City, Missouri, USA 64108

Library of Congress Control Number: 2010924007

First edition, first printing
9781935362357

Printed in the United States of America
by Walsworth Publishing Co., Marceline, MO
To order copies, call StarInfo at
(816) 234-4636 and say "Books."

ACKNOWLEDGEMENTS

It would not have been possible for me to write this book without the help and guidance of many people. First of all, my family has been wonderfully patient and supportive of all my crazy ideas and plans. I could not do anything without them!

Thanks to my children: Sarah and Tim, who keep the business flowing; Seth & Erin and Ben & Katie who help with everyday details; Jesse, Jordan and Schuyler who keep me going and are willing to do any menial task; and Talia for her sewing, organizing and good advice. But most of all, I wish to express my appreciation to my husband, Randy, for believing in me and picking up the slack around here where I fall short.

I also want to thank the members of Family Pieces, for sharing their time, talents, quilting, piecing, recipes, knowledge and for coming to an extra retreat just so I could write this book. There are too many of them to mention here by name, but you can get to know all of them in the pages of this book. They are my inspiration.

I am grateful to all the good folks at *The Kansas City Star,* for putting up with me while I learned the ins and outs of writing a quilt book. They have been unbelievably patient! And many thanks to my editor, Kent Richards—for his good humor, great skills and vision. With his help, and the rest of *The Kansas City Star,* team, this is a project I can truly be proud of.

Contents

Foreword

BY APRIL PRICE

This book is about magic. The magic of fabric and thread and creation.

But it is also about another kind of magic, less tangible perhaps, but no less real. The magic of quilt retreats.

Nearly twelve years ago, my Aunt Jill and her sister started our annual family quilt retreat. And from the very beginning, it was about more than just quilting. A few years ago Stephen Drucker wrote about how easy it is to sweep away traditions, "All it takes is one broken link–from mother to daughter, from country to city–and a little bit of hard-earned wisdom valued for hundreds of years is gone forever."

This is why we quilt and especially why we have quilt retreat. We are a society of women bound together by blood and love and quilt squares, joyfully keeping the traditions of our mothers, even if we do it on modern equipment. Beyond the patterns and the skills we learn, there is something eternal about sitting in a room with your grandmother, your aunts, your mother, your sisters, your babies, and putting pieces of fabric together into something beautiful and warm. Women have been doing this for generations, long before us. These are old traditions and we are links in a great maternal chain.

One year I had to fly to quilt retreat. I took my little baby and my sewing machine on the plane with me. The man I sat next to asked me, "What is that?"

"A sewing machine."

And then he said, incredulous, "Do you know how to use it?"

I smiled. "Sure."

"I didn't know they still made those."

And then he looked at me, a very young mother with a baby in my arms, and shook his head. I know he was thinking, "I didn't know they still made those…you know, women who have babies and pack them around the country

to go sewing with their aunts." It made me feel like I was preserving something valuable, maybe even sacred.

But we aren't preserving something just for the sake of history, or just for the sake of craft. As we piece and quilt and bind, we are preserving and strengthening our families, stitching our lives together, binding the generations to each other, and being comforted by the warmth of shared experience. We believe in family and quilt retreat allows us to find our place, where we belong and where we are needed, and reminds us of who we really are.

Not long ago, my cousin gave birth and lost her sweet baby just before our retreat. We sat together, with tears streaming, our scissors and our needles still, as we learned of her great loss. And then we did the only thing we could to help. We made a little quilt, nine patches and snowball blocks in soft blue and white, stitching out our thoughts and prayers, to comfort her in her grief, to add our tears to hers, to let her know that she was not alone.

Quilt retreat is more than just projects and fabric and new skills. It is the sweetness of shared creation, the blessing of life-long friendship, and the miracle of belonging. It is my favorite time of year. I have been stitched together with these women forever, their joys and sorrows are mine. And the beautiful quilts we create are only a symbol, a very lovely token, of the actual, eternal ties of love that bind us together.

I told you, it's magic.

—*April Price*

April at the most recent quilt retreat.

About the Author

Jill began designing quilts almost as soon as she started making them. Her creative spirit and affinity for working with fabrics result in a fresh take on traditional quilt making. She has an eye for color and pattern and loves to soften her designs with the swirls and curves of appliqué. Jill loves to share her quilting knowledge with others and has been teaching classes for over 10 years. She launched her design business, Jillily Studio in 2008 and has been busy ever since. Her designs have been featured in several quilting publications, including: *American Patchwork* and *Quilting, Quilter's Home,* and *Quilts.* She recently developed an appliqué basting glue, Appli-Glue for the quilting industry.

In addition to teaching and creating notions and patterns, Jill designs fabrics for Henry Glass Company. Her first fabric line, *"Meet Me in the Meadow,"* will soon be followed by *"Elizabeth's Letters"* and *"Thistledown."* Many more design ideas are bouncing around in her head waiting to be turned into beautiful fabrics.

Jill and her sisters, from left: Margaret Brockbank, Susan Deaton, Jill Finley, Judy Torgerson, Tori Spencer, and Jane Madsen.
Below: Scenes from Jill's studio.

Jill is blessed with a wonderful family. She and her husband, Randy, are the parents of seven children, three of whom are married, and Jill and Randy have four wonderful grandchildren. There is always a party of some kind going on at the Finley home!

The Finleys live in Highland, Utah—surrounded by the beautiful scenery of the nearby mountains and canyons—the perfect setting for Jill's creative enterprise.

At the recent Family Pieces retreat, attending members worked on their own versions of "Candied Pretzels." (See page 28.)

What this book is about...

Humans are creative beings. We are all blessed with the simple desire to make our surroundings beautiful and better than before. Some of us have to reach farther down to find the creative spark, but it is there. I am hoping that this book will inspire you to create something special—be it a quilt, a gift, or a relationship with other creative women. It can make your life beautiful!

No matter where you are or what you are working on, it is definitely more fun to share it with someone. I have always loved getting together with friends and family. There is nothing better than sharing the creative process with those you love. Several years ago, my sisters and I started a family quilt retreat. From the humble beginnings of only 8 of us our first year, Family Pieces has grown to a group of 38…sisters, mothers, daughters, aunts, cousins, and **quilters**.

We come from all levels of quilt making. Some of us are beginners and some are very accomplished. Some of us only quilt once a year and some of us are churning out quilts all the time. Even though we are not all avid quilters, every year for one glorious weekend in April, you will find us all together—Stitched Together.

Gathered from points around the country, we come to share something that has become special to us. It started as a way to preserve the art of quiltmaking, and has grown to be much more. We have found a way to build relationships based on a common goal and a family thread. The love which binds us together is born of being together. These are women who may have known each other only by the Christmas card they send or the occasional family function that draws a few of us to the same event. But now we share something more than just a family tie. We share the sleepless nights, mounds of chocolate, stories, mistakes, and quilting triumphs at Quilt Retreat.

We watch as the small chunks of fabric we cut come together into beautiful finished projects. We do not all have the same taste or style. And that is the fun part—seeing the same project from the eyes of thirty different personalities. It really does accentuate the uniqueness of each quilter.

The pages of this book are filled with ideas for you. Plan a retreat or just an afternoon to get stitching with friends. Make some gifts or work on a project with a group to give to someone special. Share what you make, what you know, and most importantly—what you are.

Planning A Retreat

A retreat can be just a few quilters or a large gathering of stitchers. Whatever your group becomes, it will need a little planning. After you determine how long you can be together, you can choose a project to work on. We have done our family retreat many different ways. Sometimes we all work on our own projects, and sometimes we have a selection of short classes. But by far, our favorite part is when we work on the group project. At the end of the retreat, we go home with a little bit of everyone in our finished quilt top. Working together is satisfying because we share the work, and have fun at the same time. As our retreat has grown, we have adjusted our typical schedule so we can be more flexible. We also have the challenge of hosting quilters with a wide variety of styles. This makes it important to offer several different classes and options. Here are some elements you will want to consider including in your retreat.

INVITATIONS

This sets the stage for the great event to come! Make your invitations interesting and fun so everyone will be looking forward to being together. Choose a theme for your retreat. All the elements such as classes, assignments and door prizes can relate back to the theme. Even your project can be theme related. Your invitations will introduce the theme and explain the format and schedule so participants can know what to expect. Include an RSVP or Sign Up for attendees to send back to you along with any fee you may charge. Make it easy, so they can quickly fill it out and send it back!

Invitations create excitement about the upcoming retreat. **Left:** Stacks of registration packets await the arrival of the quilters!

REGISTRATION

It is fun to have everyone "check in" when they arrive. It makes it feel official and gives everyone an overview of the event. We like to greet the quilters with a "Registration Packet" filled with all the necessities: schedules, class instructions, patterns, sleeping arrangements and food assignments. This "Registration Packet" has included other fun items such as a charm for our bracelet, a particular notion we might need for the project, books, fabric kits, and of course,

Planning A Retreat

chocolate. It is presented beautifully in a box or bag or basket labeled with each quilters name.

Jane helps Rosie show her work at the trunk show.

CLASSES

Depending on the group project that you choose, you may have some extra time for small optional classes. These are technique classes or simple projects which can be completed in a few hours. Here are a few ideas: appliqué techniques, aprons, bags or purses, baby blankets, pillows, pin cushions, needle or scissor case, wool felting, skirts, etc. The possibilities are endless! We usually offer several classes, and the quilters can choose two or three to attend. It is also good to offer an "Open Sewing" class where a quilter can bring her own project to work on.

TRUNK SHOW

This has become a favorite event at our retreat. We love to see the work that has been going on all year while we were apart. This is usually the first time we get a peek at the finished quilts from previous years. Each quilter adds her own "flair" to a project to make it her own. Sometimes we will see the same quilt several years in a row, each time

Above. Quilts from the trunk show are displayed as we go. **Right:** Nicole plating the Orange Rolls we made. (See page 94.) Hey look, she's wearing the Sunny Side Up Apron! (See page 102.)

showing a different stage done. (The appliqué is done, the top is set together, the quilting is done, and of course, finally, the binding is done.)

FOOD

There are several ways to do food for a group. It will depend on your group size and cooking facilities. We like to keep the costs down, so we usually do all our own cooking. One or two quilters will plan the menu and do the shopping for all the food. Then we are each assigned a meal to prepare and clean up. Some of the prep work can be done before we arrive, making meal time quick so we can get sewing! You can also plan to have each quilter bring some part of a meal. Catering or eating out is also an option. Either way, someone will need to be in charge of food to get everything organized.

One night right before our annual quilt retreat I was working on preparing classes and handouts. My grandson Isaac, who was visiting that week, asked what I was doing. I told him that I was going to have lots of ladies here for our retreat. His eyes got really big, and he said, "Do they get to have lots of treats?" From the mouths of babes…how true, how true. You can't hold a retreat without the treats. We have found that there is no shortage of treats or snacks at retreat, even if we don't assign it. It somehow magically appears. Imagine that!

We always have wonderful food and everyone shares in the work of putting meals on the table. I am glad to be able to share a few of our favorite recipes from past retreats.

GROUP PROJECT

The group project is what binds us together. When I look back on all the quilts we have made at retreat, I can see all the quilters who worked on these projects with me. Each quilt is a bundle of memories.

It is important to involve everyone in the process, no matter what the skill level may be. Assign the simpler blocks to beginners, or have them work on a team with more experienced quilters. This is an opportunity to teach as you go. Even experienced quilters can benefit from learning another method or technique. Include a little bit of instruction time as the Group Project begins so that everyone understands the techniques in the project. To accommodate different tastes, sometimes we offer 2 different colorways of the same project.

DOOR PRIZES/GAMES

Who doesn't like to win a prize! We always have a prize for everyone, which we give out during the retreat. There is usually a game or contest associated with the prize. Sometimes we fill out a questionnaire and guess who said what. Other times we guess who brought what fabric, or give a prize based on the number of quilts finished in a year. It can be as simple as drawing a name out of a hat. The games we play allow us to get to know one another better. They are short and simple, allowing us more time to play with our fabric!

Quilting Together

A quilting retreat is a unique experience. Sewing machines humming, the chatter of conversation, stacks of beautiful fabric, tables filled with snacks…and quilters. Many quilters. A small group in the center of the room is laughing hysterically. A steady stream of boxes filled with food and supplies are being carted in from the cars.

"Did anyone bring a long extension cord?" as the lights flicker.

"Unplug the iron."

And then there are the quilters…a collection of individuals with varied experiences and stashes, pattern collections and abilities, filling the room with quilting knowledge.

It's like the quilting version of the Mayo Clinic. Someone here knows how to paper piece. One quilter is an expert on appliqué. Someone else owns every quilting gadget known to man. Someone over there can tell you if you should use the red border or the green border. Another quilter knows where to find that fabric line, and how much the store has left. See, get that many quilters into one place, and you have just exponentially increased your combined quilting knowledge. And it gets even better. It's like that saying…

"The whole is greater than the sum of the parts."

Our purpose in having quilt retreat is three-fold. We want to preserve and promote the art of quiltmaking, teach new skills, and strengthen our relationships with one another.

We share the work and the fun. We do projects that involve everyone. We can work in teams or on our own. We can share fabrics, or blocks, or rows. As each quilter gets her assignment done, she will jump in to help those who are still working. (Even pressing for someone can really help.) As the group project progresses, excitement grows. No one can wait to see the whole thing put together. It's great to have every quilter go home with her own quilt top, or at least the blocks to make the quilt top!

When all the cutting and cooking and seaming and pressing and eating and sleeping (very little) are done, we go home with our quilt projects in hand, new techniques in mind, and the memories of being together.

Can't wait for next year!

A whole roomful of quilters with all their equipment and supplies. That's much more fun than quilting alone!

Square It, Share It, Flair It!

Half the fun of quilting with others is sharing. We love to do projects that involve everyone. The "Square It, Share It and Flair It" method describes it perfectly. When you see these symbols in the project instructions, you'll know what to do!

SQUARE IT

Press and trim your fabrics or blocks as needed to make sure they are nice and square. Check to be sure you have the right size including seam allowance. If you are signing your blocks, do it now. (See page 32.) Get them ready to share.

SHARE IT

Place all the fabric pieces or completed blocks on a table stacking each quilter's in a group. Now every participant will go through and take the number of blocks or fabrics needed to make her quilt. It doesn't matter how many quilters you have or how many blocks you need. As long as everyone brings enough to complete one project, there is enough to share or swap with others in the group. Every quilter will get (X) blocks or fabrics because she brought (X) blocks or fabrics.

For example, in the Carousel Quilt, (page 34) you need nine blocks. So you may have 22 quilters, but each will get only (9) blocks because she will make (9) blocks. We have used contests or drawings to determine who gets to choose first. It works out well if each quilter only picks one block each round. Then everyone gets a chance at her favorite.

FLAIR IT

Each quilter gets her blocks and setting pieces and puts her own quilt together. She can embellish if she likes, (with appliqué and other fun stuff) or just keep it simple. Some designs have more room for the "flair." For example, the Wildflower Melody Quilt (page 64) has a controlled or more formal look because one person purchased all the fabrics. So these quilts will look very similar. In contrast, A Walk in the Park (page 22) has a lot more variables since only the green fabric is shared. The setting borders and appliqué (or not) is chosen by the quiltmaker.

SNIPPETS

Throughout the book, you will find "Snippets" of information—special hints to make your quilting adventure more successful. Watch for these little bits of wisdom gained from all of the mistakes I have made, and the experience of 30+ quilters!

About Fabric and Borders

CHOOSING FABRICS

Sometimes it is overwhelming to pick all the fabrics needed for one project. There are so many wonderful choices at our quilt shops today, and fabric is readily available online as well. How do you get the right combination? Go with what you love, but use some guidelines to make it more interesting:

• Always use good quality 100% cotton quilting fabrics. There is a big difference between the goods you get at a big box store as compared to your local quilt shop. You may even find similar prints but the thread count and yarn strength will be much higher at a quilt shop. When you are putting many hours of work into your quilt you want your fabrics to be high quality!

• Use more than one fabric of each color. In other words, if your design needs a red fabric, use several different ones. It adds a lot of interest and depth. Much more fun to work on, too.

• Make sure you use a variety of scale (size of design), style (type of design), and visual texture (fabrics that look smooth vs. having a texture or pattern).

• Keep some contrast in the value of the fabrics. Value refers to the lightness or darkness of a color. This will make your design pop! Many quilters think that choosing different colors means that they will have contrast in their quilt. But even opposite colors can be the same value. To have contrast, you need light and dark of various colors.

• Try not to just use all fabrics from the same fabric line. Although they are beautiful, and designed to go together, your finished quilt will tend to look "flat." That is because they are by the same designer, and consequently have the same style and tone. Choose a few you love from one line and go on a hunt to find other fabrics that compliment your selections and make it more interesting. This trick alone will make your creation unique and reflect your style.

• When you introduce a new color or fabric into your design, use it in more than one place, so it looks like it belongs there. If, when you get to the outside border, you decide to use a print or color that doesn't relate to the rest of the quilt, it will look like you couldn't find anything to match, or ran out of fabric. However, if you use that same fabric somewhere else in the quilt, it will "belong."

• Keep your quilt balanced. Step back from your work and check to see if you have distributed your design elements equally. Scatter your darks vs lights throughout the quilt. The same is true of scattering colors, and design concepts. Large pieces and small pieces need to be mixed or the texture of your quilt will be unbalanced. And no one wants an unbalanced quilt!

• Lastly, audition your selections. Before you make a purchase, check the fabric in good light, and from a distance as well as up close. Sometimes, what you think will work in the store doesn't actually work when you get home. (*Oh, darn, I need more fabric!*) Do a final audition on your design wall. Hang a piece of each fabric and step back. I like to look at it through a reducing lens such as a peep hole viewer, or a camera lens for a better perspective. Sometimes just leaving the room and coming back later with "fresh eyes" helps.

A NOTE ABOUT BORDERS

The border sizes given in the instructions for each quilt are mathematically correct. If your piecing was perfect, and if fabric never did stretch, and if your machine didn't feed the fabrics at different rates, well, then it would work perfectly! But that is a lot of ifs! So, it is wise to measure your quilt center through the vertical center and the horizontal center to make sure you are in the ballpark. If there is a discrepancy in your quilt top size as compared to the instructions, greater than ½", change your border size to match your quilt top before you cut.

I like to use the mathematically correct sizes, because I check my block sizes as I go, and this keeps my quilt square. The block or section sizes are given in my instructions as you go along. Use these measurements to make sure your blocks and sections fit together perfectly!

Foundation Piecing

Foundation piecing is a great way to do unusual angles and is very accurate. It is kind of an "upside down and backwards" method, so if you haven't tried it, it may seem awkward at first, but you will soon be sewing up a storm!

SUPPLIES
Copies of Foundation patterns
Fabrics cut to size as
    instructed in cutting section
    of pattern
Washable Glue stick

Begin by making copies of each foundation pattern included. You can make copies on a copy machine or by tracing, or by sewing along the lines in a stack of papers, without thread in your machine. To make the reversed patterns, request "mirror image" on your copy machine, or turn pattern over and trace on the back side if you are making copies by hand. Transfer all the numbers on each section. Use light-weight paper to shorten your stitch length to make it easier to remove the paper from your blocks.

NOW BEGIN THE SEWING:

1. Each section on the foundation is numbered. Begin with section 1. Note which piece is called for in the cutting instructions. Turn your paper foundation over with the printed side down. Place the assigned fabric piece over the section. Hold the paper up to the light to see that the fabric completely covers the section with at least ¼" seam allowance past all the lines. Use a dab of washable glue stick to hold this first piece in place. The fabric will be attached to the **wrong** side of the foundation.

2. Now you are going to add section 2. Note which fabric is called for in section 2. Place that piece on top of the piece in section 1, RST (right sides together). Overlap the line between sections 1 and 2 by about ¼".

3. Holding the fabric in place, turn your foundation over so that you now see the printed side. Sew on the line which is between section 1 and section 2. You will be sewing on the right side of the paper, with the fabrics underneath.

4. Trim the seam allowance to ¼". Open up fabric 2 and press. Check to see that it covers section 2 completely and has a seam allowance by holding it up to the light.

5. Continue adding each piece of fabric to the wrong side of your paper foundation in numerical order. Always add the new piece with RST on top of the adjacent previously placed pieces, and sew on the line between sections. When the line between sections does not go all the way across the foundation, it will end at a dot. Begin at this dot and do a small backstitch or knot to start.

6. When you have sewn all the pieces for one foundation, trim the block on the solid outside line using a ruler and rotary cutter. (The dotted line is the seam line.)

7. Remove the paper foundation: Score gently along the sewn seams to break the paper with your seam ripper or awl. Gently pull the paper off being careful not to stretch the seams.

Note: Just one pattern in the book uses this method. Wildflower Melody on page 64 features two foundation pieced blocks. These instructions are simply an overview of the process. If you need additional information on this method, there are many good sources available in books, classes, and online.

Appliqué the Jillily Way

I love the look of appliqué. It can add so much to a quilt. All those curves and interesting shapes add just the right touch to the sharp, crisp lines of a pieced quilt. I avoided it for years because I thought it was too hard. But I have found that appliqué can be very easy and fun. This method makes it accessible to every quilter. Anyone can learn it, so don't be afraid to try.

1. Trace appliqué patterns on the dull side of freezer paper. Transfer solid lines and dotted lines. Reverse shapes if called for.

2. Place pattern on top of two additional layers of freezer paper. Put all layers shinny side down. Iron the papers together so that the pattern is now 3 layers thick.

3. Cut out on the solid line and just outside of the dotted lines, so you can see where they are.

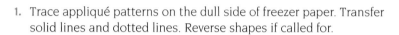

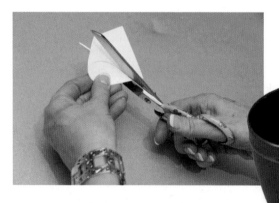

4. Place the pattern shinny side down on the wrong side of the fabric. Iron in place. The pattern will stick to the fabric.

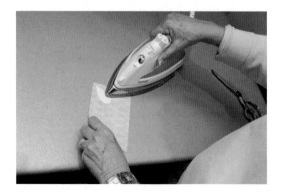

Basic Appliqué Supplies: Front: thimble pads, tailor's awl, stencil brush, Jillily Studio Appli-Glue, cotton thread, hand needles, scissors. **Back:** cup, spray starch, iron.

5. Cut around the pattern leaving a scant ¼" seam allowance beyond the solid lines. You do not need to add seam allowance to the dotted line edges. They do not need to be turned under since they will be underneath another piece. Clip inside curves if needed, about ⅛". A sharp inside point, like on the top of a heart shape, will need to be clipped all the way to the pattern. BUT before you clip, put a tiny drop of a no-fray product on the fabric where you will need to cut. This will prevent the fabric from unraveling.

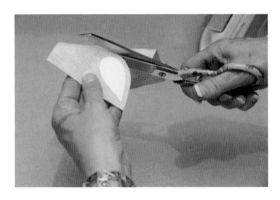

6. Spray some starch (or sizing) into a cup. It will foam up, and then liquefy. Use a small stencil brush to "paint" the seam allowance with spray starch.

7. Take the appliqué piece to your ironing board. Use a tailor's awl or seam ripper to hold the appliqué piece so you don't get burned. With a hot dry iron, press the wet seam allowance over the paper pattern. Remember not to turn the edges along dotted lines.

If you are doing a piece that has a sharp point such as the tip of a leaf, just press one side of the leaf, then the other side of the leaf, and leave the extra fabric, or 'flag,' sticking out on the end. **Do not** trim off the flag. Do not worry about turning the flag under yet.

8. Let the piece cool and remove the freezer paper pattern. The edges will be turned under crisply and stay in place. The freezer paper pattern can be used again many times. Follow the appliqué placement guide of the pattern and place the prepared appliqué pieces on the quilt starting from the back and working forward. (Place in the order they are numbered.) Glue baste in place with Jillily Studio Appli-Glue. This glue has a long precision tip so you can reach under your pieces without disturbing their placement to glue them down. Do not use too much glue, just a tiny dot every ½"–1" or so along the seam allowance of the appliqué piece. I like to be sure that the glue is not too close to the folded edge of the appliqué (so that I don't have to sew through it) but still on the seam allowance (so that it doesn't come through to the right side of the fabric.)

9. When making vines or stem, I always use a bias tape maker. Cut the strips about ⅛" wider than double the finished size. This insures that there is enough fabric to turn under nicely. I also use starch on my bias vines. Lightly spray the starch on the cut strip before you pass it through the bias tape maker. If you do it after, the moisture will undo the pressed folds. This makes the bias tape very crisp and easy to work with. It also helps it keep it's shape when you press it into a curve. Use Jillily Studio Appli-Glue to baste your vines in place.

Snippet

> I prepare all of the appliqué pieces and glue them all on to the quilt block at the same time. That way I am ready to stitch and do not have to consult the pattern again or stop to prepare another piece.

At this point you are ready to stitch. You can stitch by hand or machine. I love to hand stitch because it is so beautiful and it is a portable project. I can work on it while I am spending time outside of my sewing room. Perfect for waiting rooms, and watching football, etc. (There is a lot of time between plays!) Hand stitching can help you make use of small bits of time otherwise wasted. However, sometimes there just isn't time to hand appliqué, or you may want a project to have a different look. For these occasions, I stitch my appliqué by machine, but I still prepare the pieces the same way so that I have no raw edges. Here are the instructions for the two stitching methods.

HAND STITCHING

1. Stitch the appliqué pieces in place using thread that matches the appliqué, not the background. Use a good quality cotton thread. (I love Aurifil, because it is fine and yet strong and very smooth.) Use a fine, good quality needle so that your stitches don't show. (I love the Bohin brand appliqué needles, size 11.)

2. Hold your appliqué project with the appliqué piece toward you and the edge that you are stitching on away from you. Move from right to left, if you are right-handed and left to right if you are left-handed.

3. Stitch in an invisible stitch by coming out of the appliqué on the fold and going into the background with your needle entering a tiny bit under the appliqué edge. Travel your needle while it is under the background, then come up and out of the appliqué fold again.

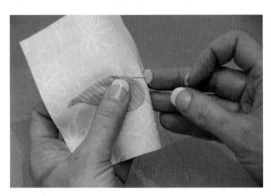

4. When you come to a point, and you have a 'flag' still sticking out, sew down one side of the appliqué all the way to the point. For the last ½" use closer stitches. Bring your needle out at the very tip of the point on the appliqué piece, and gently pull to "sharpen" the point. Now take your needle and gently fold the "flag" under the appliqué and against the back "wall" of stitching you just did on the adjacent side. Stitch down the next side using closer stitches for about ½".

5. Stitch all your appliqué pieces to the background. Press from the back side, if needed, on a soft ironing cover. Your pieces will be crisp and will puff up a little as you quilt around them with the look of beautiful needle-turned appliqué.

MACHINE STITCHING

1. First, if you have any appliqué pieces with flags sticking out at the point, these need to be turned under. Use a needle or an awl to slide the flag under and glue baste in place.

2. You can stitch by machine with a small (~⅛") zig zag stitch. Use matching thread or monofilament in clear for light colored appliqués or smoke for darker appliqués. Experiment with the thread to get the look you want. Use a size 70 or 75 machine needle so that the holes it makes will be small.

3. Start with your needle down in the background right next to the appliqué piece. Zig zag onto your appliqué and back into the background. Stitch around all the edges of your appliqués, including both sides of your stems and vines.

4. If you want a more decorative look, use a machine blanket stitch with either matching thread or contrasting thread.

5. Straight stitching close to the edge of the appliqué pieces is also an option. Try it out before you use it on your prepared quilt top to see if you like the look. I used this method on the "All Dressed Up" runner on page 50. Actually, I did the stitching after the batting and backing were layered with the runner top. That way I did the appliqué stitching and the quilting at the same time! I added more quilting after the appliqués were all stitched in place.

Fabric Exchange

The tables in the center of the room are piled high with squares cut from hundreds of different fabrics. It is our first "fabric exchange." Who would believe that all these different fabrics could come together in any sensible way! But it can work! After all the fabrics were arranged, we took turns choosing 10 fabrics at a time, until each quilter had 120 squares. We had everything there from Civil War to Amy Butler. Different quilters chose different fabrics. Some used all different styles, and some limited their selection to certain colors, or styles. There was a great deal of competition to get the favorite fabrics!

A fabric exchange is one way to share and still have control over the look of the finished quilt. To get a good variety of fabrics to choose from, you can adjust the number of fabrics each quilter brings to share. If you have a small group, have each quilter bring several fabrics. If there are many quilters in your group, they may only need to bring one fabric. The following projects are perfect for a fabric exchange. Start with the "Square It" and "Share It." Then you can get sewing and add your own "Flair It."

A Walk In The Park

FINISHED SIZE: 58" X 58"

A "fabric exchange" project. Everyone bring one green fabric; "Square It" (cut it into squares) then "Share It" (exchange the fabrics) and "Flair It" (piece your quilt center and add borders as you like.) I am including the pattern for the appliqué I used on my borders. When Erin Finley pieced her version of this quilt, she opted to use a large scale print for the borders instead of doing appliqué. (See page 27.) We both used ric rac to embellish the finished quilt.

CUTTING INSTRUCTIONS

From Cream background: (33) 5" squares
From Greens: (33) 5" squares (Add these to the "Share It" table and each quilter will take a variety of fabrics to total (33) squares.)
From border fabric: (8) strips, 7½" x width of fabric: piece as needed and cut to make:
(2) 7½" x 18", (2) 7½" x 32", (2) 7½" x 39", (2) 7½" x 53"
From Green final border: (6) strips, 3" x width of fabric, piece as needed and cut to make:
(2) 3" x 53", (2) 3" x 58"

For Appliqué:

Stems: Green fabric, cut into (24) bias strips 1⅛" wide (these strips will be about 20" long)
A leaf: (4) Green, (4) reversed Green
B leaf detail: (4) Light Green, (4) reversed Light Green
C petal: (12) Red
D center: (4) Green
E center detail: (4) Light Green
F bud: (24) Red
G bud base: (24) Green
Yo-yos: (17) Red

SEWING INSTRUCTIONS

1. Draw a diagonal line on the back of each 5" cream square from corner to corner.

2. Place a cream square on top of a green 5" square, with the right sides together. Sew ¼" away from the marked line, on both sides.

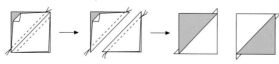

FABRIC REQUIREMENTS

½ yard Green for blocks (to share)
⅔ yard Green for appliqué stems
⅛ yard total Light and Dark Greens for leaves
⅓ yard total Reds for appliqué and yo-yos
½ yard Cream background for blocks (each quilter chooses her own)
1 ¾ yard border fabric – Cream with Red print (each quilter chooses her own)
⅝ yard Green for final outside border (each quilter chooses her own)
3 ½ yards backing
½ yard Red for binding
10 yards Green medium size ric rac

Other Supplies

½" bias tape maker
Basic appliqué supplies, see page 16

A Walk In The Park

You will have one left over hour glass block — use it to make a label for the back of the quilt! It is fun to have everyone who exchanged fabrics sign your label.

3. Cut apart on the drawn line. Press each finished half-square triangle with the seam allowance toward the green. Pair (33) cream with (33) green to make (66) half-square triangles.

4. Draw a diagonal line on the back of (33) of the half-square triangles connecting the two unsewn corners. The line will be perpendicular to the seam line.

5. Place two half-square triangles right sides together with a drawn line on top. Have the cream half of each block against the green half of the other block. Nest the seams together tightly. Sew as before on both sides of the line, ¼" away.

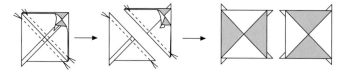

6. Cut apart on the drawn line to make hour glass blocks. Make (66) hour glass blocks.

7. Trim each block to 4" square. Make sure that the seams go right into the corner before you trim.

8. Arrange blocks in rows of (5) across, with (5) rows down, using a total of (25) blocks. Stitch the blocks together in each row and stitch the rows together. See Assembly Diagram.

9. Your center panel is done. It should measure 18" x 18".

Flair IT ▶ Add your borders and do the appliqué if desired. The appliqué instructions follow the border instructions, however, I like to finish the appliqué on each border before sewing on the next border.

10. Add the first border: Sew the (2) 7½" x 18" borders onto the sides of center panel. Press seams toward border. Sew the (2) 7½" x 32" borders on to the top and bottom of the quilt center. Press seams toward border.

11. Add the pieced border: Sew (9) hour glass blocks in a row to make the side borders. Make (2). Sew on to the sides of the quilt. Sew (11) hour glass blocks together in a row to make the top and bottom borders. Make (2). Sew onto the top and bottom of the quilt.

12. Add the next border: Sew the (2) 7½" x 39" borders to the sides of the quilt. Sew the (2) 7½" x 53" borders to the top and bottom of the quilt.

13. Final border: Sew the (2) 3" x 53" green borders to the sides of the quilt. Sew the (2) 3" x 58" borders to the top and bottom of the quilt.

APPLIQUÉ

1. Prepare the (24) 1⅛" wide bias strips by feeding them through the Clover brand bias tape maker, ½" size. This will fold the edges under. Shape the bias strips as shown on the placement diagram. Baste in place with Jillily Studio Appli-Glue.

2. Prepare appliqué pieces as described in "Appliqué the Jillily Way." (page 16) Use the Appliqué Placement Diagrams to arrange pieces on quilt top. Baste in place with Jillily Studio Appli-Glue. Stitch all appliqués and stems in place.

3. Prepare (17) yo-yos: Cut from red fabric using the yo-yo pattern. Fold the raw edge around the circle a scant ¼" to the wrong side. Hand stitch around the circle with a short basting stitch, (about ¼" long) while holding the folded edge in place. Keep your stitches about ⅛" from the fold edge. Use a strong quilting thread in a matching color.

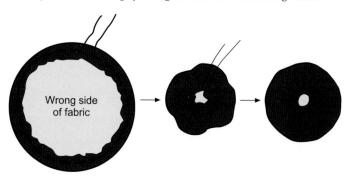

Wrong side of fabric

Draw up the threads tightly to close the circle. Tie off. Don't cut the threads yet. Push the center (small gathered circle) of the yo-yo down and pull the sides out to create a nice symmetrical yo-yo. This is the top of the yo-yo. Re-thread the tied off threads in your needle and pull them through to the back of the yo-yo. Knot in place. Place according to Quilt Diagram using (13) in the quilt center and (4) in the outside corners of the quilt. Baste in place with Jillily Studio Appli-Glue. Stitch.

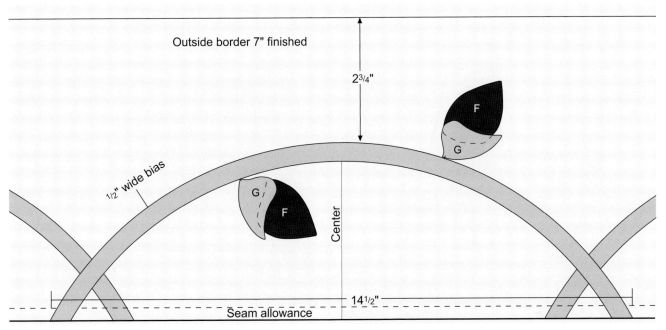

|← 24½" →|

Inner border

E
D
C
A
B
B(R)
A(R)

½" bias width

Appliqué Placement Diagrams

Outside border 7" finished

2¾"

½" wide bias

F
G
G
F

Center

14½"

Seam allowance

Appliqué Placement Diagrams

4. Place ric rac over the seams between hour glass blocks and borders. Top stitch with matching thread, turning at the corners going all the way around each border. Turn under the end of the ric rac where they meet.

5. Layer, quilt and bind.

Assembly Diagram

A Walk In The Park

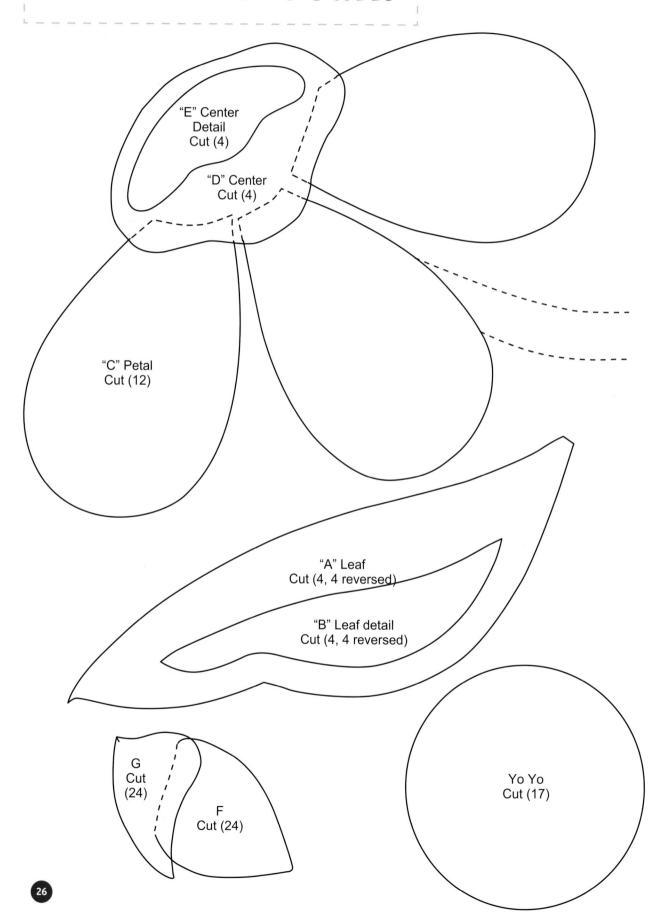

"E" Center Detail Cut (4)

"D" Center Cut (4)

"C" Petal Cut (12)

"A" Leaf Cut (4, 4 reversed)

"B" Leaf detail Cut (4, 4 reversed)

G Cut (24)

F Cut (24)

Yo Yo Cut (17)

A Walk in the Park, 2009. 58" x 58"
Pieced and appliquéd by Jill Finley;
quilted by Tori Spencer.
Second version: Pieced by Erin Finley;
quilted by Tori Spencer.

Candied Pretzels

FINISHED SIZE: 63" X 75"

This is a fabric exchange quilt. Every quilter brings her own fabric for background, "candies," and borders. She brings fabric "pretzels" to share. This is the quilt we did at our last retreat. Many of the retreat photos in the book show this quilt in various stages of completion. You can see a variety of finished quilt tops in photos throughout the book.

CUTTING INSTRUCTIONS
From Background fabric: (14) strips, 5" x width of fabric, (4) strips, 2" x width of fabric
From Contrast fabric: (18) strips, 2" x width of fabric
From Accent fabric: (6) strips, 1½" x width of fabric
From Border fabric: (80) 2" squares, (6) strips, 5½" x width of fabric

SEWING INSTRUCTIONS

> **Share it** — Place all the 2" Contrast fabric strips (for the pretzel sticks) on a table with each stacked in a group. Depending on how many quilters you have, choose from 1 to 6 strips at a time, until every quilter has 18 strips.(Each quilter will have come with (18) strips of her fabric, and she now swaps it with the other quilters for more interest and FUN!)

1. Pair up (14) 2" Contrast fabric strips with your own (14) 5" background fabric strips. Sew each set together along the long edge. Press toward the Contrast fabric.

2. Slice the strip sets into 6½" slices. This will make 6½" squares. Cut (80).

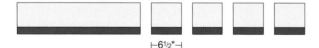

├─6½"─┤

3. Draw a diagonal line on the back of (80) 2" squares of border fabric from corner to corner. Place a 2" square on one corner of the 6½" square from step 2, noting the orientation in the diagram. Sew on drawn line. Trim seam allowance to ¼". Press open. Make (80).

Snippet

When you are doing a scrappy group project, you may want to control the color choices a little bit by giving some rules, such as: "pastels only," or "'30's prints," or "brights." We controlled our colors by sending each quilter a swatch of focus fabrics that included lots of colors. She could then choose a coordinating fabric to match the focus fabric. She may or may not use the same focus fabric in her borders.

FABRIC REQUIREMENTS
2 ¼ yards Background
1 ⅛ yards Contrast for pretzels (this one is to share)
⅓ yard Accent fabric for stop border
1 ¼ yards Border fabric (also for candies)
⅝ yard binding
3 ¾ yards backing

Candied Pretzels, 2010. 63" x 75" Pieced by Talia Finley; quilted by Virginia Gore.

Candied Pretzels

4. Arrange your blocks in rows as in diagram with (8) across and (10) down.

5. Sew the blocks in each row together.

6. Sew the rows together.

 Each quilter can add borders (or not) as desired. Maybe she will do a little appliqué in the border, it's up to her.

Here are the directions for how Talia finished her quilt:

7. Prepare the stop border: Using the 1½" wide strips, piece together and cut (2) borders 60½" long and (2) borders 50½" long.

8. Sew the 60½" borders on to either side of the quilt center. Sew the 50½" borders on to the top and bottom of the quilt center.

9. Prepare the main border: Using the 5½" border strips, piece together and cut: (2) borders 62½" long and (2) borders 60½" long

10. Sew the 62½" borders on the sides of the quilt. Sew the 60½" borders on the top and bottom of the quilt. Press toward borders.

11. Prepare the outside pieced border: You will be using the (4) remaining 2" contrast fabric strips. You can swap these if you want more variety. Slice the 2" contrast strips into (44) 3½" pieces and (2) 2" squares. Slice the 2" background strips into (44) 3½" pieces and (2) 2" squares.

12. Alternate the background 2" x 3½" pieces with Contrast 2" x 3½" pieces in a long row, sewing together on the short edge. Put (24) pieces together for each side border, and sew to the quilt. Put (20) pieces together for the top and bottom with the 2" squares on each end. Sew to quilt.

13. Layer quilt top with batting and backing. Quilt and bind.

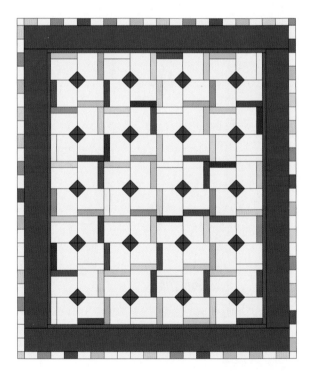

Assembly Diagram

CARAMEL AND CHOCOLATE PRETZELS

Every year before Quilt Retreat, my niece Rachel makes these yummy (and beautiful) dipped pretzels. She wraps them individually and ties them with a pretty ribbon. Then they are tucked inside the box of goodies which is given to each quilter as they arrive for the yearly festivities. Rachel has shared her recipe with me, so I will share it with you!

Rachel's Caramel and Chocolate Pretzels

1/2 cup butter
2 cups brown sugar
1 can sweetened condensed milk
3/4 cup light corn syrup
1 tsp. vanilla
1—2 lbs. dipping chocolate
8 oz white or dark chocolate for decoration
candy sprinkles for decoration (optional)
25-35 large pretzels

Line a large cookie sheet with parchment paper. In a medium saucepan, bring butter, brown sugar, sweetened condensed milk and corn syrup to a rolling boil over medium heat, stirring constantly. While continuing to stir, boil for 5-7 minutes. (Until it reaches soft ball stage.) Remove from heat and let sit. When caramel has stopped bubbling, add 1 tsp vanilla and stir. Working quickly, dip large pretzel sticks in caramel and lay on parchment paper (do not use wax paper). Let sit until cool.

Melt dipping chocolate in a double boiler. Dip caramel coated pretzels in chocolate and put back on parchment paper. Let chocolate cool. Melt white or dark chocolate, drizzle over caramel chocolate pretzel sticks or add candy sprinkles if you like. Enjoy.

Block Exchange

In a block exchange project, each quilter will make her own block multiple times to exchange with others. This is the most common way to work together. Sometimes you are all working with the same pattern for the block and your own fabrics. You could also each do different blocks to exchange. Sometimes it is nice to have the same background fabric to give the finished quilt continuity. Block Exchange projects are excellent candidates for signature quilts. Just have every quilter sign her own blocks before she "squares it." Use a pen designed to be colorfast and safe for the fabric. To stabilize the fabric and make it easy to sign, iron a piece of freezer paper on the back of the block. Make sure you don't sign in the seam allowance.

The following projects are good for a block exchange. To control the color choices, one person may purchase all the background or focus fabrics, and have each quilter bring some block fabrics. Or your group may want a scrappy look and just give a few color "suggestions" or rules to make each quilt. Have fun working together!

Carousel

FINISHED SIZE: 56" X 56"

Charming piecing and sweet appliqué draw your eye around and around this beautiful quilt. To get the variety of fabrics in the reds and pinks, we do a block exchange. Each quilter will bring a red and a pink fabric, which coordinate with your focus fabric. She will piece all her pinwheel blocks using these fabrics and then the blocks will be exchanged. Using the same background and focus fabrics lend a more formal look, but you could also do them scrappy.

CUTTING INSTRUCTIONS

Focus Fabric: (1) 10" x 10"; cut in half diagonally twice to yield 4 small triangles, (6) 9" x 9"; cut each square in half diagonally to yield (12) large triangles, (4) 4½" x 4½"

Accent Fabric: (5) strips, 2" x width of fabric

Assorted Pinks: (27) 3" x 3" (9 sets of 3 each), (24) 2½" x 4½"

Assorted Reds: (27) 3" x 3" (9 sets of 3 each), (28) 2½" x 4½"

Cream background: (1) 10" x 10"; cut in half diagonally twice to yield 4 small triangles, (4) 9" x 9"; cut in half diagonally to yield (8) large triangles, (4) 8½" x 8½", (18) 3" x 3", (84) 2½" x 4½", (112) 2½" x 2½", (5) strips, 3" x width of fabric

For Appliqué:

From ½ yard Green, cut for stems: (14) ⅝" bias strips (strips will be about 24" long)

Assorted Greens: (12) Leaf 12, (12) Leaf 13, (4) Base 9, (4) Base 10, (4) Base 11

Assorted Reds: (4) Berry 14, (4) each of Petals 1, 2, 3, 4, 5, 6, 7, and 8

Assorted Pinks: (8) Berry 14

RETREAT FABRIC REQUIREMENTS

Group purchase: Cream background, Focus Fabric (Buy enough for every quilter. Give samples to each quilter so she can make her fabric selections coordinate.)

Each quilter bring: ½ yard pink, ½ yard Red, and ⅓ yard Accent fabric for stop border (and her own backing and binding.)

FABRIC REQUIREMENTS

2¾ yard Cream background

¾ yard Focus Fabric for setting

⅓ yard Accent Fabric for stop border

½ yard Reds

½ yard Pinks

½ yard binding

3⅓ yards backing

Appliqués

½ yard Green

¼ yard total assorted Greens

¼ yard total assorted Reds

¼ yard total assorted Pinks

Supplies

¼" bias tape maker

Basic appliqué supplies, see page 16

Carousel hangs on the wall while the companion runner, **Merry-Go-Round**, is displayed on the coffee table. (See page 42.)

Carousel

SEWING INSTRUCTIONS
Make the Blocks
(Instructions are for one block, make 9 blocks total.)

1. Draw a line on the back of (2) pink 3" squares in a set, and two cream 3" squares, from corner to corner diagonally. Pair up the pinks with two red 3" squares in a set. Pair up the remaining pink 3" square and 3" red square with the 3" cream squares.

2. Place the squares right sides together. Sew a seam ¼" away from the drawn line, on both sides. Cut the squares apart on the drawn line. This will make two half-square triangles. Press them open with the seam allowance toward the dark fabric. Now trim each square to 2½".

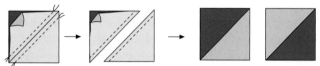

Trimming the block after you have sewn will allow you to make crisp and accurate half-square-triangles with the seam right in the center. It takes a little longer, but it is worth it because the pieces all go together so nicely with no cut off points.

3. Sew the other squares in the same manner. You will have (8) half-square-triangles: (4) pink/red (2) pink/cream and (2) red/cream

4. Following the diagram, sew sets of two pink/red squares together and press in opposite dirctions so that the seams will nestle when they are sewn. Now sew the pairs together 4-patch style to make a pinwheel square.

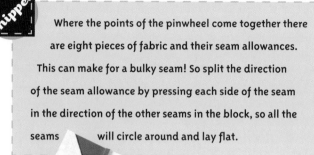
Where the points of the pinwheel come together there are eight pieces of fabric and their seam allowances. This can make for a bulky seam! So split the direction of the seam allowance by pressing each side of the seam in the direction of the other seams in the block, so all the seams will circle around and lay flat.

5. Sew a 2½" x 4½" background piece to the sides of the pinwheel square. Press seam toward background.

6. Sew a red/cream square to one end of each remaining 2½" x 4½" cream piece. Sew a pink/cream square to the other end. Note the orientation of the half-square triangles. Press seam allowance away from the half-square triangles.

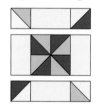

7. Sew these units onto top and bottom of the pinwheel block. Press the seams away from the pinwheel block. Blocks should measure 8½" x 8½".

Each quilter adds her blocks to the "Share It" table, then takes a total of (9) blocks to use in her quilt.

Make the Setting Blocks

8. Pair eight large cream triangles with eight large Focus fabric triangles with the right sides together. Sew along the long diagonal edge in a ¼" seam. Handle these pieces gently, as you are sewing on a bias edge, and it can easily stretch. Carefully press the seam allowance toward the focus fabric. Trim each large half-square triangle to 8½" x 8½".

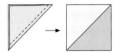

9. Pair the (4) small triangles of focus fabric with (4) small cream triangles. Place right sides together. Sew in a ¼" seam along a short side. Carefully press seam allowance toward the focus fabric.

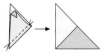

10. Pair the triangle units pieced in Step 2 with the remaining large focus fabric triangles. Place them right sides together, matching the center seam with the center of the large triangle. Sew the long edge together in a ¼" seam. Press toward the focus fabric. Trim each block to 8½" x 8½".

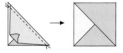

Construct the Quilt Center

11. Lay out your blocks according to the diagram. Sew the blocks together in rows.

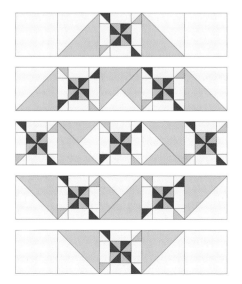

12. Sew the rows together.

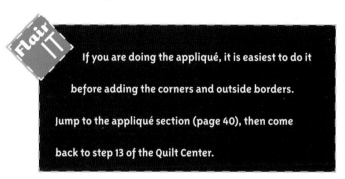

If you are doing the appliqué, it is easiest to do it before adding the corners and outside borders.

Jump to the appliqué section (page 40), then come back to step 13 of the Quilt Center.

13. Place the (4) 4½" squares of focus fabric onto the corner blocks of the quilt with right sides together. Sew diagonally from corner to corner. Trim seam allowance to ¼". Press toward the corner.

Carousel

Borders

14. Using the (5) 2" strips of accent fabric, cut (2) stop borders 40½" long, and (2) stop borders 43½" long. Depending on the width of your fabric, you may have to piece these borders, or you may be able to get them out of one strip.

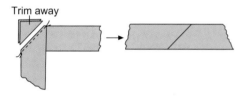
When you piece strips to make a border, use a diagonal seam and the piecing will not be as noticeable or as bulky. Lay the strip ends right sides together and perpendicular to one another. Sew from the corner of the top strip to the corner of the underneath strip in a diagonal seam. Trim seam allowance to 1/4" and press. Voila!

Trim away

15. Sew the 40½" stop borders to the top and bottom of the quilt center. Press toward border.

16. Sew the 43½" stop borders to the sides of the quilt center. Press toward the border.

17. From the (5) 3" strips of cream fabric, make (2) borders 43½" long, and (2) borders 48½" long. Sew the 43½" borders to the top and bottom of the quilt center. Sew the 48½" borders to the sides of the quilt center. Press seams toward borders.

18. Make the flying geese: Draw a diagonal line from corner to corner on the back of (104) 2½" cream background squares. Place one of these squares on top of a red 2½" x 4½" rectangle right sides together.
Sew on the drawn line. Trim seam allowance to ¼". Press triangle open. Sew another 2½" cream background square onto the other side of the red rectangle. Trim and press open. Make (28) red flying geese. Use the pink 2½" x 4½" rectangles to make (24) pink flying geese.

19. Piece together (6) pink flying geese alternated with (5) 2½" x 4½" cream background pieces in a long strip. Make four. To two of the strips add a 2½" cream background square to each end. To the other two strips, add a 2½" x 4½" cream background rectangle to each end.

Make 2

Make 2

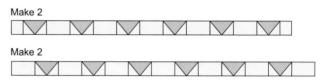

20. Sew the strips with the squares on the ends to the sides of the quilt center. Sew the remaining two strips to the sides of the quilt. (Arrange all strips with the pink flying geese pointing **in** to the center of the quilt.)

21. Piece together (7) Red flying geese alternated with (6) 2½" x 4½" cream background pieces in a long strip. Make four. To two of these strips add a 2½" cream background square to each end.

Make 2

Make 2

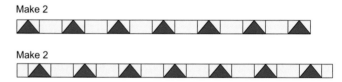

22. Sew the red flying geese strips to the top and bottom of the quilt. Sew the two strips with squares on the ends to the sides of the quilt. (Arrange the flying geese to point **out**.)

23. Layer top with batting and backing. Quilt and bind.

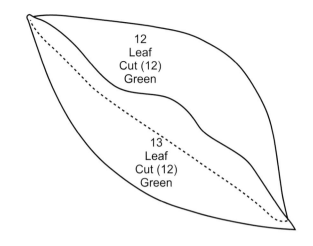

12
Leaf
Cut (12)
Green

13
Leaf
Cut (12)
Green

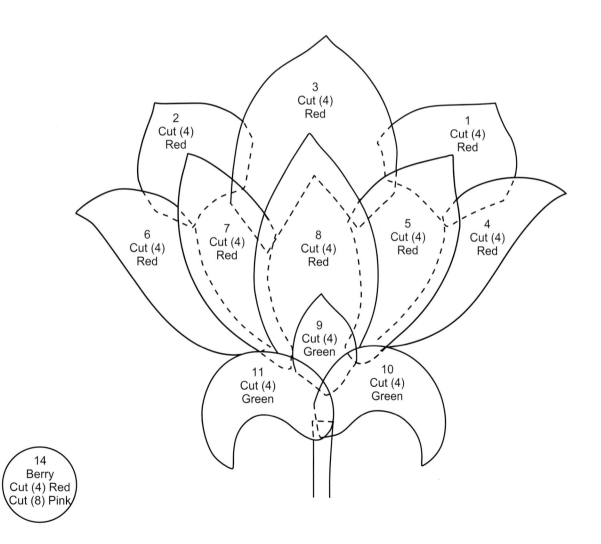

3
Cut (4)
Red

2
Cut (4)
Red

1
Cut (4)
Red

7
Cut (4)
Red

8
Cut (4)
Red

5
Cut (4)
Red

6
Cut (4)
Red

4
Cut (4)
Red

9
Cut (4)
Green

11
Cut (4)
Green

10
Cut (4)
Green

14
Berry
Cut (4) Red
Cut (8) Pink

Carousel

When I am creating curvy vines or stems using bias strips I use this trick to make the vines all consistent: I draw the pattern onto plain paper with a pencil and place the paper on the ironing surface. I place the bias along the line and follow it with a hot iron, creating each curve and loop. Sometimes the curves are so tight that it may take two or three passes with the iron to get the right bend in the bias. If you are making a mirror image vine, just place it on the pattern with the wrong side up.

APPLIQUÉ

1. Prepare all the appliqué pieces by turning the edges using the Appliqué the Jillily Way method found on page 16.

2. Layout the applique as shown in the Assembly Diagram. Glue baste in place using Jillily Studio Appli-Glue.

3. For stems, use the (14) ⅝" bias strips. Pass them through a ¼" bias tape maker to fold the edges under. Press them into shape using a hot iron following the Assembly Diagram.

4. Stitch appliqué pieces by hand or by machine. The ends of the stems can be tucked into the seams by undoing a few stitches and re-stitching.

Assembly Diagram

Carousel, 2009. 56" x 56" Pieced and appliquéd by Jill Finley; quilted by Peggy Shadel.

Merry-Go-Round

FINISHED SIZE: 20" X 54"

This is the perfect project for your retreat if you love the look of the Carousel Quilt, but need something a little faster. Only four blocks to make here, and no appliqué.

CUTTING INSTRUCTIONS

Focus fabric: (1) 10" x 10" square, cut in half diagonally twice (from corner to corner), (3) 9" x 9" squares, cut in half diagonally once. (4) 2½" x 2½"

Cream background: (8) 3" x 3", (16) 2½" x 4½", (60) 2½" x 2½"

Assorted Reds: (12) 3" x 3" squares (four sets of three), (14) 2½" x 4 ½", (2) 2½" x 6½"

Assorted Pinks: (12) 3" x 3" squares, (four sets of three), (14) 2½" x 4 ½"

Accent fabric: (3) 2" x width of fabric strips, (5) 1½" x width of fabric strips

SEWING INSTRUCTIONS

1. Follow the instructions in Carousel Quilt under "Make the Blocks" for steps 1-7 on page 36. Make (4) blocks.

 Square blocks to 8 ½" x 8 ½" and share with other quilters so that each quilter takes (4) blocks.

2. Lay out blocks and large setting triangles, which were cut from 9" focus fabric squares. Place the short side of the triangle against the block. Sew together in rows. Trim row to be 8½" wide. (The blocks will be the correct size, but the setting triangles are a tiny bit larger, and will need to be trimmed after sewing.)

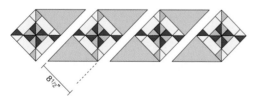

3. Now sew the rows together.

4. Sew a small setting triangle, cut from the 10" squares of focus fabric onto each corner along the long edge. You will have extra fabric on the outsides.

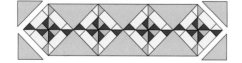

FABRIC REQUIREMENTS
⅓ yard Focus fabric
⅝ yard Cream background
⅓ yard total of Red fabrics
⅓ yard total of Pink fabrics
½ yard Accent fabric (Dark Green)
⅜ yard binding (Dark Green)
1 ⅔ yard backing

Merry-Go-Round, 2009.
20" x 54" Pieced by
Margaret Brockbank;
quilted by Peggy Shadel.

Merry-Go-Round

5. Trim your center leaving ¼" beyond the points for seam allowance. The center should measure approximately 11½" wide by 45½" long.

6. Using the accent fabric 2" strips, piece together and cut to make: (2) strips, 45½" x 2", (2) strips, 14½" x 2"

7. Sew the long accent strips onto the long sides of the runner center. Press seam toward border.

8. Sew the short accent strips onto each end of the runner center. Press toward border.

9. Make the flying geese using the (14) 2½" x 4½" red and (14) 2½" x 4½" pink and (56) 2½" squares of cream background. Follow the instructions in step 5 of the border section of Carousel Quilt on page 37. Make (28) flying geese.

10. Sew (12) flying geese together along their short sides to make a strip, randomly placing red and pink flying geese. Make two of these borders and sew to the long sides of runner. Refer to Assembly Diagram.

11. Make two "fat geese" with the 6½" x 2½" red rectangles. Sew a 2½" cream background square on each end in a corner triangle. This "goose" will not have a point in the center, (and probably won't get off the ground,) but it **will** fit the quilt!

12. Make the end borders by sewing a flying geese unit to either side of a fat goose unit. Then sew a 2½" focus fabric square on each end. Make two end borders and sew them onto the ends of the runner. Refer to Assembly Diagram.

13. Piece the final borders of accent fabric from the 1½" strips to make: (2) 1½" x 52½", (2) 1½" x 20½".

14. Sew the long borders onto the sides first, then the short borders on each end. Press toward the borders. TaDah!

15. Layer top with batting and backing. Quilt and bind.

Assembly Diagram

The Best Thing About Quilt Retreat

...when you discover you can **finally** sew a straight line! — **Tori**

...when **anything** can either make you laugh hysterically or bawl your eyes out. — **Amy B.**

...our fabulously silly and fun family! Oh, and chocolate. — **Maika**

...seeing **all** the talent the ladies in the family have. — **Katie F.**

...hearing the hysterical giggles that start after 10 pm. — **Nicole**

...swapping everyone's funniest or craziest stories from the past year. — **McKelle**

...Quilt Retreat is my favorite holiday. — **Melissa**

...being surrounded by love and laughter and yards of beautiful fabric. —**Nicole**

...getting back your round robin after not seeing it for 9 months and loving it to death. — **Tori**

...seeing all the great projects at the Trunk Show. — **Jill**

...I feel so blessed to be a part of all of this. It makes me so happy to know that all of you have such different and silly personalities. — **Hillary**

...the retreat seems to go on all year when doing Round Robin! — **Judy**

...while planning the next Quilt Retreat, we couldn't recall past retreat memories without laughing! We are a funny bunch of women! — **Christine**

Dressed to the Nines

FINISHED SIZE: 78" X 78"

This quilt uses a lot of blocks, so you may want each person in your group to bring more than one medium or dark fabric. If you have a lot of quilters, you will have enough variety with each bringing only one fabric. We did not have any rules on fabric choice on this one. The pieces are so small that all styles of fabrics can be used successfully!

CUTTING INSTRUCTIONS

From Medium to Dark fabrics: (15) 1½" x width of fabric, (66) 2½" squares

From Background: (12) 1½" x width of fabric, (64) 3½" squares

From Stop border fabric: (6) strips, 2½" x width of fabric — piece as needed and cut for stop border: (2) 2½" x 52", (2) 2½" x 56"

From Setting fabric: (66) 2½" squares, (9) 9½" squares, (3) 14" squares — cut in half twice diagonally, (2) 7¼" squares — cut in half once diagonally, (14) strips, 5½" x width of fabric — piece as needed and cut for borders: (2) 5½" x 54½", (2) 5½" x 64½", (2) 5½" x 68½", (2) 5½" x 78½"

SEWING INSTRUCTIONS

1. Using the 1½" strips of background and dark fabrics, create the following strip sets by sewing together along the long edge. Press to the dark.

Strip set A – make (6)

Strip set B – make (3)

RETREAT FABRIC REQUIREMENTS

Group purchase: Background fabric used in the blocks. Bring enough for every quilter.

Each quilter bring: Medium or Dark fabric to make her blocks to share and the pieced border. She will also bring her own fabric for setting and borders.

FABRIC REQUIREMENTS

1 ⅛ yards Medium or Dark fabric (for blocks to share)

1 ¼ yards Cream dot (for blocks) background fabric

3 ¾ yards Cream print for setting fabric

½ yard Green for stop border

⅝ yard Green for binding

4 ⅝ yards backing fabric

2. Cut strip sets into 1½" slices. Keep your ruler perpendicular to the seam lines. Cut (160) from strip set "A" and (80) from strip set "B."

3. Sew slices together to make (80) 9-patch blocks.

> Square up blocks to 3½" x 3½".

> Place all the finished blocks from each quilter in sets on the table. Each quilter will choose (80) blocks. Place all the cut 2½" medium or dark squares on the table. Each quilter will choose (66) 2½" squares.

4. Sew blocks into a large 9-patch using the 3½" background squares alternated with the shared 3½" blocks. Sew them together in rows first, then sew the rows together. The large 9-patch should measure 9½" square. Make (16) large blocks.

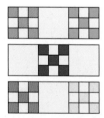

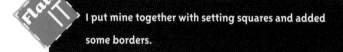

> I put mine together with setting squares and added some borders.

5. Lay out quilt center together in diagonal rows following diagram. Use the quarter-cut setting triangles on the edges and the half-cut triangles in the corners.

6. Sew rows together. Measure your quilt center from top to bottom. The stop borders you have cut are generously sized. Measure your quilt center and cut (2) down to this length. Sew onto the sides of quilt.

7. Measure from side to side and cut the remaining borders to this length. Sew onto top and bottom. This is a coping border to allow for size differences due to setting blocks on point. Now measure again and trim stop borders as needed for quilt to measure 54½" x 54½".

8. Add the first border. Sew the 5½" x 54½" border to the sides. Sew the 5½" x 64½" border to the top and bottom.

9. Sew the pieced border: Make (2) strips alternating (16) med/dark 2½" squares with (16) setting fabric 2½" squares. Sew to sides of quilt. Make (2) strips alternating (17) med/dark 2½" squares with (17) setting fabric 2½" squares. Sew to top and bottom of quilt. Refer to Assembly Diagram.

10. Now add the final border. Sew the 5½" x 68½" borders to the sides of the quilt. Sew the 5½" x 78½" borders to the top and bottom of the quilt.

11. Layer top with batting and backing. Quilt and bind.

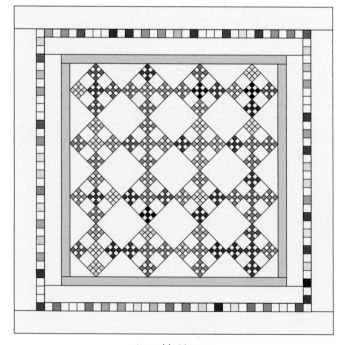

Assembly Diagram

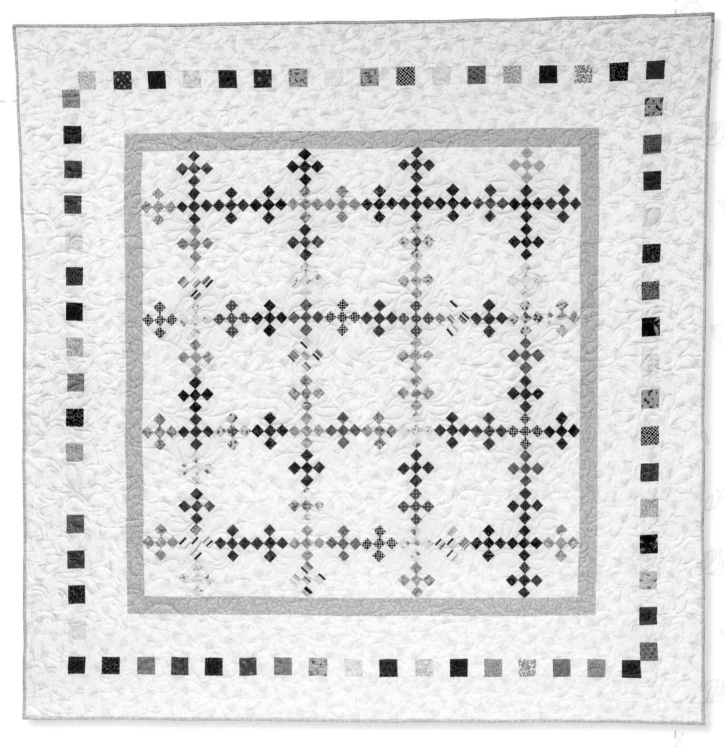

Dressed to the Nines, 2009. 78" x 78" Pieced by Susan Deaton; quilted by Tori Spencer.

All Dressed Up

FINISHED SIZE: 17" X 42"

This quick project will be much more fun after you exchange blocks with everyone in your group. Have one person buy all the background fabric, or you can each bring your own to make it very "scrappy." Finish it off with the optional appliqué.

CUTTING INSTRUCTIONS

From Medium or Dark print: (1) 45" x 19" for backing, (5) 1½" x 25" strips
From Background: (2) 9½" x 16", (2) 9½" x 8", (1) 12" x 12", (4) 1½" x 25", (12) 3½" squares
For Appliqué: (8) bias strips, ⅜" wide for vines, (10) of pattern 1 (Leaf) from green, (12) of pattern 2 (Berry) from blue, (12) of pattern 3 (Flower) from reds.

SEWING INSTRUCTIONS

1. Using the 1½" strips of background and dark fabrics, create the following strip sets by sewing together along the long edge. (Press to the dark.)

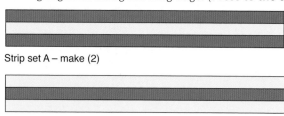

Strip set A – make (2)

Strip set B – make (1)

2. Cut strip sets into 1½" slices. Keep your ruler perpendicular to the seam lines. Cut (30) from strip set "A" and (15) from strip set "B".

3. Sew slices together to make (15) 9-patch blocks.

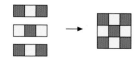

FABRIC REQUIREMENTS

1 ¼ yard Medium or Dark print (this one we will share and use for backing)
1 yard Light background
¼ yard for binding
⅔ yard Green for vines and leaves
⅛ yard total assorted Reds for flowers
6" x 6" scrap Blue for berries

Other Supplies:

¼" bias tape maker
Basic appliqué supplies, see page 16

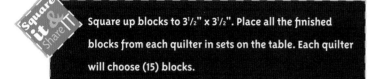

All Dressed Up

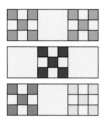 Square up blocks to 3½" x 3½". Place all the finished blocks from each quilter in sets on the table. Each quilter will choose (15) blocks.

4. Sew blocks into a large 9-patch using the 3½" background squares alternated with the shared 3½" blocks. Sew them together in rows first, then sew the rows together. The large 9-patch should measure 9½" square.

5. Prepare the setting pieces: Place the background 9½" x 16" horizontally on your cutting board as shown. Measure from the lower left corner to a point 12½" inches away on the bottom edge. Place your ruler on that point with the 45 line on the edge of the fabric so that your ruler is on a diagonal. Cut the fabric into (2) pieces. See figure 1. Repeat with the other 9½" x 16". Place the background 12" square on the cutting board. Cut in half diagonally from corner to corner. See figure 2.

45°

12½"

Figure 1

12"

Figure 2

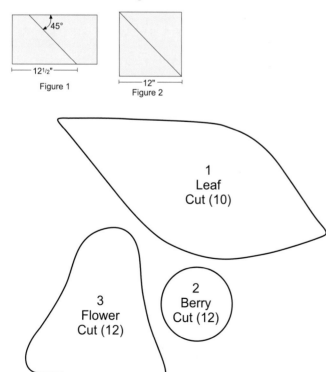

1
Leaf
Cut (10)

3
Flower
Cut (12)

2
Berry
Cut (12)

6. Lay out your runner with the 9-patch blocks on point. Use the prepared background setting pieces (from step 5) and the background 9 ½" x 8" pieces. Place each 9-patch block in the center of a row following diagram. The excess fabric will be trimmed later. For now, just make sure you match up the points on the small 9-patch units with each other as you sew the rows together.

7. Trim the runner to 17" x 45".

 Add the appliqué if desired.

APPLIQUÉ

1. Prepare all the appliqué pieces as described in "Appliqué the Jillily Way" on page 16.

2. Feed the ⅝" bias strips through a ¼" bias tape maker. Follow the placement diagram to curve your bias vines loosely along the outside edge of runner. Place the starting edge of each new vine section under another vine to cover all raw edges.

3. Place all flowers, leaves and berries as in the Placement and Assembly Diagram. Glue baste all pieces with Jillily Studio Appli-Glue.

4. Stitch in place by hand or machine. Quilt and bind.

Placement and Assembly Diagram

All Dressed Up, 2009.
17" x 42" Pieced
and appliquéd by
Jill Finley; quilted
by Jill Finley.

Garden Rows

FINISHED SIZE: 60" X 72"

Plant your garden early to get your rows blooming! Seeds, shoots, flowers and garden stakes are all part of this neatly laid out garden plot. Garden Rows is based on simple blocks repeated in rows. Exchange the rows just as you would blocks. Depending on the expertise of your quilters, you may decide to combine a few simple rows for one quilter to do, or have two or more quilters work on row 4 with the appliqué, since it is more time consuming. Many different fabrics are used in each color "position" to add to the visual texture and interest. To get a variety of fabrics, you could assign each quilter a color of fabric to bring for the group as well as a row to stitch.

CUTTING INSTRUCTIONS

From Blacks: (4) 4½" squares (Row 1), Eight sets of (2) 3½" squares (Row 2), (24) 2½" squares (Row 3), (1) of appliqué pattern 6 (Row 4), (32) 2" squares (Row 5), (12) 3" squares (Row 7)

From Background prints: Four sets of: (2) 4½" x 6½" and (4) 4½" x 2½" (Row 1), (8) 12½" x 5½" (Row 4), (20) 2½" squares (Row 6), (4) 2½" x 8 ½", (12) 3" squares (Row 7)

From Reds: Two sets of (6) 2½" squares (Row 1), (8) 2½" x 6½" (Row 3), (2) of appliqué pattern 1 (Row 4), (2) of appliqué pattern 3 (Row 4), (4) of appliqué pattern 4 (Row 4), Five sets of (4) 4½" squares (Row 6), Two sets of: (2) 4½" x 2½" and (2) 2½" x 8½ (Row 7)

From Golds: Two sets of (6) 2½" squares (Row 1), (8) 6½" x 3½" (Row 2), (8) 2½" x 6½" (Row 3), (20) 1¼" squares (Row 6), Two sets of: (2) 4½" x 2½" and (2) 2½" x 8½ (Row 7), (2) of applique pattern 2 (Row 4)

From Greens: (8) 2½" x 6½" (Row 3), (4) bias strips, 1⅛" wide x 10" long (Row 1, optional appliqué stems), (2) bias strips, 1⅛" wide x 20" long (Row 4), (2) bias strips, ⅞" wide x 20" long (Row 4), (3) of appliqué pattern 7 (Row 1, optional Leaf), (2) of appliqué pattern 4 (Row 4), (2) of appliqué pattern 5 (Row 4), (2) of appliqué pattern 5 Reversed (Row 4), (8) 6½" x 3½" (Row 5), Two sets of: (2) 4½" x 2½" and (2) 2½" x 8½ (Row 7)

To set your quilt together as I did, cut the following: (See the **flair it** section on pg 58.)

From Greens: (4) 12½" x 2½"
From Reds: (8) 12½" x 2½"
From Golds: (4) 12½" x 2½"
From Background print: (8) 12½" x 2½"

FABRIC REQUIREMENTS

¼ yard each of 4 Reds
¼ yard each of 6 Background prints
¼ yard each of 4 Golds
¼ yard each of 4 Blacks
⅛ yard each of 6 Greens
½ yard Green for bias stems
⅓ yard of 1 Black for inner border
1 ¼ yard Green for outer border
⅝ yard Black for binding
3 ⅝ yards backing

Other Supplies:

1/2" bias tape maker
3/8" bias tape maker
Basic appliqué supplies, see page 16

Garden Rows

From Black for inner border: (6) 1 ½" x width of fabric strips, piece and cut to make: (2) 1½" x 60½", (2) 1½" x 50½"

From Green for outer border: (7) 5½" x width of fabric strips, piece and cut to make: (2) 5½" x 62½", (2) 5½" x 60½"

See "A Note About Borders" on page 14.

SEWING INSTRUCTIONS

Row 1: Stretched Star Flowers

1. Use one set of red or gold and one set of background prints for each flower. A red flower is described here. Repeat to make two red and two gold flowers for each quilt.

2. Draw a diagonal line on the back of each 2½" red square. Place right sides together on a background print 4½" x 2½" rectangle. Align corner edges. Sew across the corner on the drawn line. Trim seam allowance to ¼". Press open. This is a corner triangle. Make (2).

3. Sew a 2½" red square in a corner triangle on one corner of a black 4½" square. Sew a second 2½" red corner triangle on the opposite corner.

4. Sew the units from step 2 to the top and bottom of the unit in step 3.

5. Sew a 2½" red corner triangle on one corner of a 4½" x 6½" background print rectangle. Orient as shown. Sew a background print 4½" x 2½" rectangle to the bottom edge. Make (2).

6. Sew the units from step 5 to the sides of the unit in step 3 as shown. This is one flower block and should measure 12½" x 8½". Piece (4) blocks together in a row alternating the reds and golds.

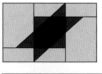

> Row should measure 48½" x 8½".

7. Add optional appliqué: Prepare the 1⅛" wide bias strips by passing them through a ½" bias tape maker, as described in "Applique the Jillily Way" on page 16. Using the photo as a guide, gently curve the bias strips into shape with a hot iron. You can turn the end near the flower under to hide the raw edge, or open the seam a little and tuck the raw end inside. Re-sew seam. Prepare leaves, glue baste all appliqués down and stitch.

Row 2: Furrows

1. Sew a 3½" black square in a corner triangle on a gold 6½" x 3½" rectangle. Trim and press open. Sew a second corner triangle using a matching 3½" black square on the adjacent corner. Make (8) blocks.

2. Sew the furrow blocks together along the short edge in a long strip.

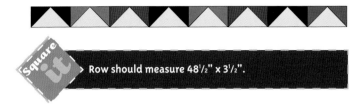

Row should measure 48½" x 3½".

Row 3: Garden Stakes

1. Sew a black 2½" square on the short end of a red 2½" x 6½" rectangle. Make (8). Repeat using the green and gold 2½" x 6½" rectangles to make (8) of each color.

2. Sew the (24) units from step 1 together along the long edges, alternating orientation of the black squares from top to bottom as shown, and placing in order: red, gold, green, red gold, green, etc.

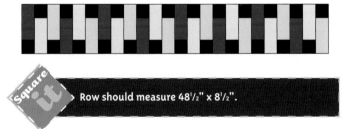

Row should measure 48½" x 8½".

Row 4: Perennials

1. Arrange the 12½" x 5½" background print rectangles in two rows of four each. Sew together along the short sides. Each row should measure 48½" x 5½".

2. Sew the two rows of background prints together. This is the base for your appliqué.

3. Prepare the appliqué pieces as described in "Appliqué the Jillily Way" on page 16. Pass the ⅞" bias strips through the ⅜" bias tape maker, and the 1⅛" strips through the ½" bias tape maker. Layout all appliqué elements on the pieced base following the Placement and Assembly Diagram. Glue baste in place. You could share your row after this step and have each quilter finish the stitching. Or if there is enough time, you could do the stitching before you exchange rows. I stitched by machine using monofilament thread (smoke color) in the top, and cotton thread in the bobbin, with a tiny zig zag, as described in the machine stitching section on page 19. It is quick and beautiful!

Row should measure 48½" x 10½".

Row 5: Seeds

1. Sew a 2" black square in a corner triangle on one corner of a green 6½" x 3½" rectangle. Trim and press open with the seam pressed toward the green. Sew a 2" black square on the opposite corner of the green rectangle, pressing in the same manner. Make (8).

2. Sew a 2" black square in a corner triangle on the remaining two corners of the same green rectangle. Press open with the seam allowance pressed toward the black. This will make it easier to sew the "seeds" together. Make (8).

3. Sew the "seeds" together along the short ends to make a long strip. Match the points of the seeds as you go, nesting the seams together.

Row should measure 48½" x 3½".

Row 6: Poppies

1. Sew a 2½" background print square in a corner triangle on one corner of a 4½" red square. Make (20) using all the 4½" red squares in the five sets.

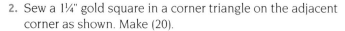

2. Sew a 1¼" gold square in a corner triangle on the adjacent corner as shown. Make (20).

3. Orient the four squares in each set as shown. Sew together the top two, then the bottom two. Press seams opposite and sew the top row to the bottom row. Make (5) poppies. Blocks should measure 8½" x 8½".

4. Use the (4) 2½" x 8½" background print rectangles as spacers between poppies and sew the row together as shown.

> Row should measure 48½" x 8½".

Row 7: Potting Flats

1. Draw a diagonal line on the back of the (12) 3" squares of background print, from corner to corner. Pair up each one with one of the (12) 3" squares of black, right sides together. Sew two diagonal seams: ¼" away from the drawn line, on each side. Cut apart on the drawn line. This will make two half-square-triangles. Trim each to 2½" x 2½". Make (24).

2. Arrange the half-square-triangles in a 4-patch, as shown. Sew the top two together, then the bottom two together. Press seams opposite. Sew the rows together.

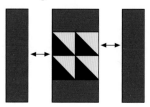

3. Sew a 4½" x 2½" rectangle of red on the top and one on the bottom of a 4-patch from step 2. Sew a red 2½" x 8½" rectangle to each side. This is one complete block.

4. Make one more block with red, two of gold, and two of green for a total of six blocks. Each block should measure 8½" x 8½".

5. Sew blocks together in a row, alternating colors: red, gold, green, red, gold, green.

> Row should measure 48½" x 8½".

> Exchange rows so that each quilter gets one of each row.

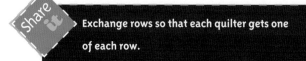

> Each quilter will put her rows together as she chooses. The instructions that follow tell you how I finished my quilt.

FINISHING:

1. Sew four 2½" x 12½" green pieces together along the short sides to make a long sashing strip. Repeat using four 2½" x 12½" pieces in each sashing strip. Make one strip of green, one of gold, two of red, and two of background prints for a total of six sashing strips. Layout as shown in Placement and Assembly Diagram and sew the rows together.

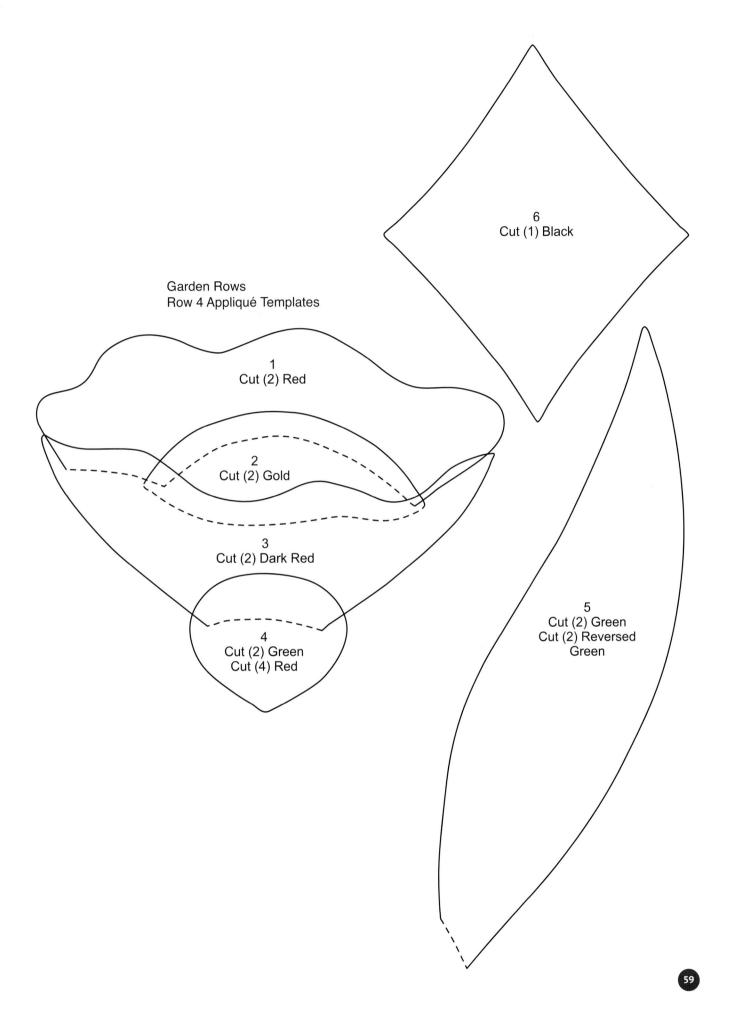

Garden Rows
Row 4 Appliqué Templates

6
Cut (1) Black

1
Cut (2) Red

2
Cut (2) Gold

3
Cut (2) Dark Red

4
Cut (2) Green
Cut (4) Red

5
Cut (2) Green
Cut (2) Reversed
Green

Garden Rows

2. Sew a 1½" x 60½" black stop border to each side of quilt. Sew the black 1½" x 50½" stop border to the top and bottom. Sew a 5½" x 62½" green border to each side. Sew a 5½" x 62½" green border to the top and bottom of quilt.

3. Layer quilt top with batting and backing. Quilt and bind. Enjoy!

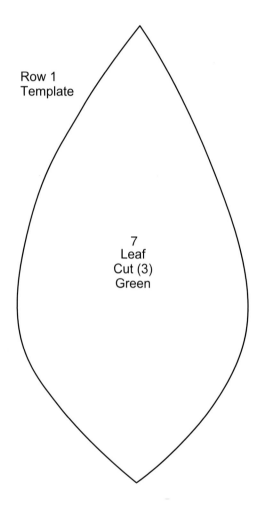

Row 1
Template

7
Leaf
Cut (3)
Green

Placement and Assembly Diagram

Garden Rows, 2009. 60" x 72" Pieced and appliquéd by Jill Finley; quilted by Peggy Shadel.

Team Work

This is possibly the most enjoyable way to quilt together! Picture it...teams of quilters working on the same section of the quilt to share with everyone. It provides the most interaction between quilters. It is a great choice when your group has varied abilities, or the pattern uses varied techniques. You may have an experienced group, but not everyone is comfortable with each technique. One year when we did a team project, I did all the fabric shopping so that all the sections of the quilt would coordinate. That was a LOT of fabric...enough for 24 quilts! Each team enjoyed a LOT of cutting and a LOT of sewing! We had chosen a fairly complicated pattern, but we were able to finish all the blocks for 24 quilts in 2 days! As I recall, this quilt involved a lot of hysterical laughter (due to lack of sleep) and even general panic when one team realized they had done half of their block backwards...24 times! Good thing I bought so much fabric!

Put together some teams at your next retreat and try one of these great projects!

Wildflower Melody

FINISHED SIZE: 62" X 81"

Imagine walking through an alpine meadow with plenty of blue sky for a backdrop and beautiful blooms scattered around you. Like a beautiful song, Wildflower Melody captures all the "notes" in a pleasing arrangement with a scalloped trim flourish on each block, and a touch of lyrical appliqué. This is a great project for using Team Work. The blocks use various techniques so you can put together teams of people who are most comfortable with each method. Each quilter in your group can go home with the whole meadow!

SCALLOPED BLOCK BORDERS

Blocks 1-9 each have the same scalloped border treatment. Instead of having this border instruction repeated with each block, it is given here. You can have each team add this border to their blocks, or make it part of the individual quilters responsibility.

Cutting: For each block, cut the following:
From Blue: (12) 1½" x 3½", (4) 1½" x 2½"
From Black: (28) 1" x 1"

Sewing:
1. Place a black 1" square on both ends of the long edge of a 1½" x 3½" blue piece. (RST) Sew diagonally from corner to corner, making a corner triangle. Trim seam allowance to ¼" and press open. Make (12).

Make 12

2. Place a black 1" square on top of a 1½" x 2½" blue piece aligning one corner, as in the diagram. Sew in a corner triangle. Make (2). Make the remaining (2) blue pieces with a black corner triangle in the adjacent corner.

Make 2   Make 2

FABRIC REQUIREMENTS

Fabrics needed for one entire quilt top are listed here so that you can plan and purchase all the fabrics needed to make each participant a quilt. The cutting instructions for each block is listed separately with the block instruction.

1 ¾ yard Medium Blue
1 ½ yard Light Blue
⅜ yard Cream
¾ yard White
2 yards Black
1 ⅓ yard Greens (I used 3 different Greens)*
1 yard Cream Print for border
⅛ yard Red
3 ¾ yards Backing
⅝ yard Binding

Other Supplies:
⅜" bias tape maker
Chalk pencil
Basic appliqué supplies, see page 16

* **You may want to set aside** any large green fabric pieces needed to cut all your bias strips first, and use the remaining pieces for applique leaves and smaller pieces. Bias strips are called for in Blocks 2, 4, 6, 8, and 10.

3. Sew (2) 3½" units from step 1 together along the short sides, matching the black triangles. Sew a 2½" unit from step 2 on each end of this border. Make (2).

4. Sew (4) of the 3½" units from step 1 together along the short sides to make a border. Make (2).

5. Sew the borders from step 3 onto the top and bottom of the finished 10½" block. (All of blocks #1 - #9.) Sew the borders from step 4 on the sides of block. Block should now measure 12½" x 12½".

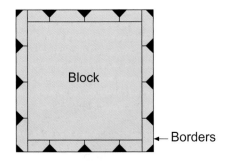

Block

← Borders

BLOCK 1: CANDYTUFT
Cutting:
From Medium Blue: (16) 2½" x 1½" for sections #5 and #6, (8) 6" x 3" for section #7
From White: (8) 2½" x 3" for section #1
From Cream: (8) 2" x 2" for section #3, (8) 2½" x 3½" for section #4
From Green: (8) 2" x 2" for section #2
From Black: (1) of Template A, Block #1 for appliqué detail

Construction:
1. Begin by making copies of each foundation pattern included. For each Candytuft Block, you will need (4) Main Foundation and (4) Main Foundation reversed.

2. Use the Foundation Piecing instructions on page 15 to sew all your pieces to their foundations.

3. Sew each completed Main Foundation to a Main Foundation reversed along seam line A. Leave the paper on for this, matching the seam lines. This will make block quarters.

4. When you have all four quarters of your block done, remove the paper foundation.

5. Sew the four quarters together, 4-patch style, with two on top, and press one way, and two together on the bottom, pressed the other way, then put the pairs together.

6. Once the block is pieced, there is a little detail of appliqué added to the center of the block. Use the piece you cut for Template A. Appliqué to the center of the Candytuft flower following the method in "Appliqué the Jillily Way" on page 16.

7. At this point, the block should measure 10½" x 10½".

8. Add Scalloped Block Borders to block following instructions on page 64.

Square it ▸ **Block should now measure 12 ½" x 12 ½".**

BLOCK 2: GOOSEBERRY WREATH
Cutting:
From Light Blue: (1) 11" x 11"
From Greens: (4) ⅞" bias strips, 15" in length (Use a fabric strip at least 12" wide to get 15" in bias. I used two different green fabrics for both the vines and leaves.), (4) of Large Leaf templates, (4) of Small Leaf templates.
From Red: (4) of Berry template

Construction:
1. Press blue 11" square in half twice to divide it into quarters. Cut an 8" circle out of paper and center it on your block. Trace around circle with chalk pencil.

2. Prepare bias strips using ⅜" bias tape maker. Use your hot iron to press the strips into shape matching the curve of the circle. Place the vines using the photo as a guide with each vine beginning under another vine and ending with a leaf so there are no raw edges. Glue baste in place using Jillily Studio Appli-Glue.

3. Prepare the Leaf and Berry pieces using the method described in "Appliqué the Jillily Way" on page 16.

4. Place all Leaf and Berry pieces as shown in photo. Glue baste in place with Jillily Studio Appli-Glue. Stitch pieces in place either by hand or machine.

5. Trim block to 10½" x 10½". Add borders to block by following instructions given in "Scalloped Block Borders" on page 64.

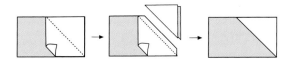
Block should measure 12½" x 12½".

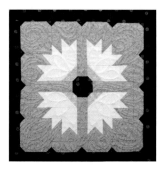

BLOCK 3: SWEET WILLIAM

Cutting:
From Medium Blue: (4) 2½" x 2½", (8) 2½" x 1½", (8) 2" x 1¾", (4) 4½" x 1 ½"
From White: (4) 1½" x 2½", (4) 1½" x 1½", (4) 3¾" x 2", (4) 2¼" x 2", (16) 1¼" x 1¼"
From Green: (4) 2" x 2"
From Black: (1) 2½" x 1½", (2) 1½" x 1", (4) 1" x 1"

Construction:
1. Place a 1½" white square right sides together (RST) on a blue 2½" x 1½" matching up edges as shown. Sew diagonally from corner to corner. Trim seam allowance to ¼". Press triangle open. This is a corner triangle. Make (4).

2. Sew the unit from step 1 to a 2 ½" blue square. Make (4).

3. Place a 2½" x 1½" of white on top of a 2½" x 1½" of blue, RST. Orient with the pieces perpendicular as shown in diagram. Sew across the corner from the corner of the blue piece to the corner of the white piece. Trim seam allowance to ¼". Press open. Make (4).

4. Sew the unit from step 3 to the unit from step 2. Make (4).

5. Sew a 1¼" white square in a corner triangle on a 2" x 1¾" blue piece as shown.

Add another 1¼" corner triangle on the adjacent corner on the long side. Make (8) of these units.

6. Sew a unit from step 5 to a 2¼" x 2" white piece joining the 2" sides with the white together. Make (4). Sew the remaining (4) units from step 5 to the 2" side of the 3¾" x 2" white pieces. Sew these pieces to the units from step 4. Make (4).

7. Sew a 2" green square in a corner triangle on the white corner of each unit from step 6. Make (4).

Wildflower Melody

8. Now add a 1" black square in a corner triangle on the green corner of each unit from step 7. Make (4).

9. Sew a black 1½" x 1" piece to the end of a blue 4½" x 1½", on the 1½" side. Make (2). Sew these long pieces between two of the units from step 8. Make (2) sections.

10. Make the center section by sewing the black 2½" x 1½" between the two remaining 4½" x 1½" pieces along the short sides. Sew this section between the two sections from step 9. The block at this point should measure 10½" x 10½".

11. Add the "Scalloped Block Borders" as described on page 64.

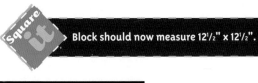

Block should now measure 12¹/₂" x 12¹/₂".

BLOCK 4: WILD GERANIUM WREATH
Cutting:
From Light Blue: (1) 11" x 11"
From Green: (2) ⅞" bias strips, 12" in length
From White: (7) of Flower template
From Red: (7) of Center template
From Green: (8) of Leaf template (I used two different greens)

Construction:
1. Press blue 11" square in half twice to divide it into quarters. Cut a 7¼" circle out of paper and center it on your block. Trace around circle with chalk pencil.

2. Prepare bias strips using ⅜" bias tape maker. Use your hot iron to press the strips into shape matching the curve of the circle. Place the vines in one circle covering the marked circle as shown in photo. Glue baste in place with Jillily Studio Appli-Glue.

3. Prepare all Flowers, Centers, and Leaves for appliqué as described in "Appliqué the Jillily Way" on page 16.

4. Place all appliqué pieces as shown in photo. You may trim away the vine underneath the flowers to reduce bulk if you like. Leave at least ¼" from edges for seam allowance. Glue baste in place with Jillily Studio Appli-Glue. Stitch pieces in place either by hand or machine.

5. Trim block to 10½" x 10½". Add borders to block by following instructions given in "Scalloped Block Borders" on page 64.

Block should measure 12¹/₂" x 12¹/₂".

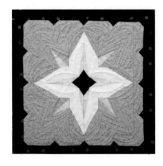

BLOCK 5: SEGO LILY
Cutting:
From Medium Blue: (8) 4½" x 3½" for section B1, (8) 4" x 2½" for section A1
From Light Blue: (8) 1½" x 5" for section A3
From White: (8) 3" x 5½" for section A2
From Green: (8) 4" x 2" (I used two different greens) for section B2
From Black: (8) 2" x 2" for section A4

Construction:
1. Begin by making copies of each foundation pattern included. For each Sego Lily Block, you will need: (4) Foundation A, (4) Foundation A reversed, (4) Foundation B, and (4) Foundation B reversed.

2. Use the Foundation Piecing instructions on page 15 to sew all your pieces to their foundations.

3. Sew each completed Foundation A to a completed Foundation B along seam line A. Leave the paper on for this, matching the seam lines.

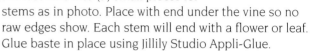

4. Sew each completed Foundation A Reversed to a completed Foundation B Reversed along seam line A. Leave the paper on for this, matching the seam lines.

5. Place the sections from step 3 right sides together with the reversed sections from step 4. Sew along seam B. This will make four quarters of the block.

6. When you have all four quarters of your block done, remove the paper foundations. Be careful not the stretch the fabric or seams.

7. Sew the four quarters together, 4-patch style, with two on top, and press one way, and two together on the bottom, pressed the other way, then put the pairs together. At this point, block should measure 10½" x 10½".

8. Add borders to block by following instructions given in "Scalloped Block Borders" on page 64.

Block should now measure 12½" x 12½".

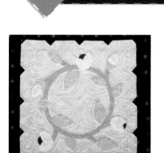

BLOCK 6: EVENING PRIMROSE WREATH
Cutting:
From Light Blue: (1) 11" x 11"
From Green: (3) ⅞" bias strips 13" long
From 2nd Green: (2) of Flower Hip template, (4) of Large Leaf template, (5) of Small Leaf template
From White: (3) of Petal #1 template, (5) of Petal #2 template
From Red: (3) of Center template

Construction:
1. Press blue 11" square in half twice to divide it into quarters. Cut a 7" circle out of paper and center it on your block. Trace around circle with chalk pencil.

2. Prepare bias strips using ⅜" bias tape maker. Use your hot iron to press (2) of the strips into shape matching the curve of the circle. Place the vines in a circle covering the marked circle as shown in the photo with each vine

beginning under the other vine and curving around, ending outside the circle with a flower on the end. Cut the last vine into (3) small pieces for stems as in photo. Place with end under the vine so no raw edges show. Each stem will end with a flower or leaf. Glue baste in place using Jillily Studio Appli-Glue.

3. Prepare the Leaf, Flower, Center, and Hip pieces using the method described in "Appliqué the Jillily Way" on page 16.

4. Place all appliqué pieces as shown in photo. Glue baste in place with Jillily Studio Appli-Glue. Stitch pieces in place either by hand or machine.

5. Trim block to 10½" x 10½". Add borders to block by following instructions given in "Scalloped Block Borders" on page 64.

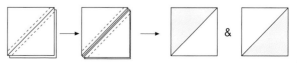

Block should measure 12½" x 12½".

BLOCK 7: DAISY
Cutting:
From Medium Blue: (4) 3½" x 1½", (4) 2½" x 1½", (12) 1½" x 1½", (4) 2" x 2"
From Green: (4) 2" x 2", (4) 2½" x 1½", (8) 1½" x 1½", (4) 1" x 1"
From White: (2) 4" x 4", (4) 4½" x 1½"
From Cream: (2) 4" x 4", (4) 4 ½" x 1½"
From Black: (1) 2½" x 2½"

Construction:
1. Draw a line on the back of each white 4" square. Pair each square with a cream 4" square, right sides together (RST). Sew ¼" away from the drawn line, on both sides. Cut apart on the drawn line. Press each square open. You will have 4 units. Trim each square to 3½" x 3½".

Wildflower Melody

2. Place a blue 2" square RST on the white side of each half-square triangle unit from step 1, aligning edges. Sew from corner to corner as in diagram. Trim seam allowance to ¼". Press open. This is a corner triangle. Make (4).

3. Sew a green 2" square in a corner triangle on the cream side of each half-square triangle. Make (4).

4. Sew a blue 1½" square in a corner triangle on a green 2½" x 1½" piece as shown. Trim and press. Make (4).

5. Sew a blue 3½" x 1½" piece to the white/blue side of each unit from step 3 as shown. Sew a 2½" x 1½" blue piece to each unit from step 4 on the short green side. Sew this piece adjacent side of previous unit. This is a corner unit. Make (4).

6. Make the center units: Sew a cream and white 4½" x 1½" pieces together along the long side. Make 4. Sew two corner triangles of blue 1½" on one end, and two green 1½" corner triangles on the other end as shown.

7. Sew a center unit between two corner units as shown. Make (2).

8. Sew a 1" green corner triangle on each corner of the 2½" black square. Sew this square between two center units on the short sides.

9. Sew the sections from step 7 on either side of the section from step 8. Your block should now measure 10½" x 10½".

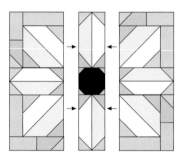

10. Add borders to block by following instructions given in "Scalloped Block Borders" on page 64.

Block should now measure 12½" x 12½".

BLOCK 8: BANEBERRY WREATH
Cutting:
From Light Blue: (1) 11" x 11"
From Green: (5) ⅞" bias strips, 13" in length (I used two different green fabrics for both the vines and leaves.) (5) of Leaf template
From Red: (3) of Berry template

Construction:
1. Press blue 11" square in half twice to divide it into quarters. Cut a 7" circle out of paper and center it on your block. Trace around circle with chalk pencil.

2. Prepare bias strips using ⅜" bias tape maker. Use your hot iron to press the vines into shape. Use (2) vines to cover

70

chalk line making a circle. Trim excess if needed.

3. Use (2) more vines to weave in and out of the circle. Press into the curvy shapes you need as you place them. Refer to photo. Cut the remaining vine into two shorter pieces filling in where needed. Place the beginning edge of each vine under another vine and ending with a leaf so there are no raw edges. Glue baste in place using Jillily Studio Appli-Glue.

4. Prepare the Leaf and Berry pieces using the method described in "Appliqué the Jillily Way" on page 16.

5. Place all Leaf and Berry pieces as shown in photo. Glue baste in place with Jillily Studio Appli-Glue. Stitch pieces in place either by hand or machine.

6. Trim block to 10½" x 10½". Add borders to block by following instructions given in "Scalloped Block Borders" on page 64.

 Block should measure 12¹/₂" x 12¹/₂".

BLOCK 9: WATERCRESS
Cutting:
From Medium Blue: (4) 3½" x 3½", (8) 1½" x 1½"
From White: (4) 3½" x 2½", (4) 2½" x 2½", (2) 3" x 3"
From Cream: (4) 3½" x 2½", (4) 2½" x 2½", (2) 3" x 3"
From Black: (4) 2½" x 2½"
From Green: (4) 1½" x 1½"

Construction:
1. Place a 2½" square of white on top of a 3½" x 2½" cream piece, right sides together (RST), matching up the corners as shown. Sew diagonally from corner to corner. This is a corner triangle. Make (2) oriented this way. Make (2) more reversed.

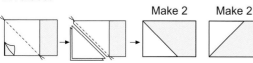
Make 2   Make 2

2. Sew the units from step 1 together on the long side as shown. Make (2).

3. Sew a 1½" blue square in a corner triangle on each cream corner of the unit. Make (2).

4. Repeat steps 1, 2, and 3 using the white 3½" x 2½" pieces with corner triangles of 2½" cream squares and 1½" blue squares. Make (2).

5. Sew a blue 3½" square to either side of the units made in step 4. Make (2). Set aside.

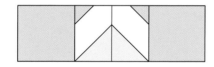

6. Using the method described in Block 7 step 1, create 4 half-square triangles using the white and cream 3" squares. Trim to 2½" square.

7. Place a black 2½" square on top of each cream/white half-square triangle. Sew across the square from corner to corner, opposite the existing seam. Orient as shown in diagram. Trim seam allowance to ¼" and press open.

Make 2   Make 2

8. Add a 1½" green corner triangle on each half-square triangle, on the black corner. Make (4).

9. Sew the four half-square-triangle units together, 4-patch style with two on top and two on bottom with all the green corner triangles meeting in the center. Orient as shown in diagram. This is the center unit.

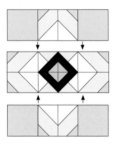

10. Sew a unit from step 3 to each side of the center unit in a row as shown.

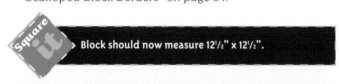

11. Sew a row from step 5 to either side of the center row to complete the block. Block should now measure 10½" x 10½".

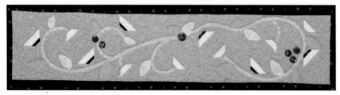

12. Add borders to block by following instructions given in "Scalloped Block Borders" on page 64.

Block should now measure 12½" x 12½".

BLOCK 10: MORNING GLORY
Cutting:
From Medium Blue: (3) strips 3¾" x width of fabric, cut strips into: (5) 3¾" x 8½", (1) 3¾" x 7", (6) 3¾" x 4½", (3) 3¾" x 3½", (7) 3¾" x 2½", (1) 3¾" x 2", (1) 3¾" x 1½"
From White: (6) 2½" x 2½", (6) 2" x 2"
From Black: (6) 1½" x 1½"
From Green: (12) 1⅛" x 1⅛"

Cutting for appliqué:
(I used two different green fabrics for the appliqué. Randomly choose your green fabrics for appliqué pieces.)
From Green: (3) ⅞" bias strips, 28" in length, (11) of Leaf A, (6) of Leaf B
From Red: (1) of Berry C, (5) of Berry D

Construction:
1. Use a pencil and ruler to draw a diagonal line from corner to corner on the back of all white squares, black squares, and green squares.

2. Place a white 2½" square right sides together on a blue 3¾" x 4½" rectangle. Align in one corner as shown, matching up the edges of each piece, and having the drawn line go across the corner. Sew on the drawn line. Trim the seam allowance to ¼" and press open. This is a corner triangle.

3. Now sew a corner triangle using a black 1½" square on the same corner. Trim and press.

4. Use a green 1⅛" square to sew one more corner triangle on this same corner. Trim and press.

5. This unit is the completed large flower. There are (6) large flowers in the block. Follow the diagram below to make the remaining (5) large flowers on the indicated blue rectangles. (The large flowers are the ones with the black stripe.) The size for each rectangle is 3¾" wide. The height of each rectangle is shown on the Assembly Diagram. Be sure to orient each rectangle to put the corner triangle on the correct corner.

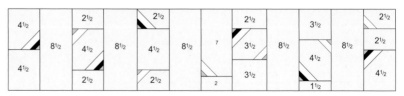

Assembly Diagram

6. Now make the small flowers using the white 2" squares and the remaining green 1⅛" squares sewn into corner triangles in the same manner. (There is no black triangle in the small flowers.) Place them on the blue rectangles as indicated in the Assembly Diagram. Be sure to orient the rectangles the correct way.

7. Lay out the block pieces following the Assembly Diagram. Sew each section together in columns, then sew the columns together.

Snippet

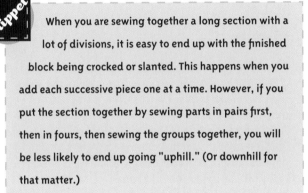

When you are sewing together a long section with a lot of divisions, it is easy to end up with the finished block being crocked or slanted. This happens when you add each successive piece one at a time. However, if you put the section together by sewing parts in pairs first, then in fours, then sewing the groups together, you will be less likely to end up going "uphill." (Or downhill for that matter.)

8. Prepare the bias vines by passing the ⅞" bias strips through a ⅜" bias maker to turn the edges under as described in "Applique the Jillily Way" on page 16.

9. Following the Placement Diagram on page 82, place the vines and shape them into the curves using a hot iron. Use one strip for the left half of the main vine, and one strip for the right half. They will not quite meet in the middle, but you will cover that area with leaves as shown. Use the third strip to make the remaining pieces of the vine as shown. Glue baste in place using Jillily Studio Appli-Glue.

10. Prepare the Leaf and Berry pieces using the method described in "Applique the Jillily Way" on page 16.

11. Place all Leaf and Berry pieces as shown in photo. Use the large berry in the center. Glue baste in place with Jillily Studio Appli-Glue.

12. Stitch pieces in place either by hand or machine.

Square it

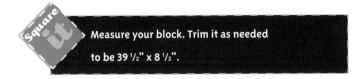

Measure your block. Trim it as needed to be 39 ½" x 8 ½".

BLOCK 11: ICELAND POPPY

This block uses so many small pieces that it is easiest to cut them and sew them in groups. The groups are: Flower Sections, Upright Bloom Sections and Branching Bloom Section. The Cutting directions and the Construction directions will be listed under these groups.

Cutting for Flower Sections:

From Medium Blue: (4) 3½" x 6½", (4) 2" x 7½", (2) 2 x 1½", (2) 3⅛" x 2½", (2) 3⅛" x 4½", (2) 2 x 2½"
From White: (4) 2½" x 2½"
From Black: (4) 1½" x 1½"
From Green: (4) 1⅛" x 1⅛", (4) 2" x 2", (2) ⅞" x 2 ½", (2) ⅞" x 4½"

Cutting for Upright Bloom Sections:

From Medium Blue: (3) 3⅞" x 4", (6) 2" x 2", (3) 2" x 2¼", (3) 2" x 3 ¼", (3) 2" x 4¾", (3) 2" x 3¾"
From White: (3) 3⅞" x 1½"
From Black: (3) 3⅞" x ¾"
From Green: (3) 3⅞" x ¾", (6) 2" x 3½", (3) ⅞" x 6½"

Cutting for Branching Bloom Section:

From Medium Blue: (1) 2½" x 5½", (1) 2½" x 3½", (1) 2½" x 2", (1) 2½" x 1½", (1) 2⅝" x 1½", (1) 2⅝" x 1¾", (1) 2" x 2¼", (1) 2" x 2", (1) 1⅝" x 3", (1) 1½" x 3⅝", (1) 1½" x 3 ½", (2) 1½" x 1½", (1) 1½" x 1", (1) 1⅛" x 2¼"
From Green: (1)⅞" x 6", (1) ⅞" x 2½", (1) 2" x 2", (2) 1⅞" x 1½", (1) 1½" x 1½", (2) 1" x 1"
From White: (1) 2 ½" x 2 ½", (1) 2" x 2", (1) 1¼" x 2½"
From Black: (1) 1½" x 1½"

Cutting for Setting Together:

From Medium Blue: (2) 2½" x 8½", (2) 1½" x 8 ½"

Construction for Flower Sections:

1. Use a pencil and ruler to draw a diagonal line from corner to corner on the back of all white squares, black squares, and green squares.

2. Place a white 2½" square right sides together on a blue 3½" x 6½" rectangle. Align in one corner as shown, matching up the edges of each piece, and having the drawn line go across the corner. Sew on the drawn line. Trim the seam allowance to ¼" and press open. This is a corner triangle.

3. Now sew a corner triangle using a black 1½" square on the same corner. Trim and press.

4. Use a green 1⅛" square to sew one more corner triangle on this same corner. Trim and press. This is a flower unit. Make (2) of these.

5. Make two more flower units with the flower on the bottom left side of a blue 3½" x 6½" rectangle as shown. (Mirror image.) Make (2).

6. Use a 2" green square to make a corner triangle on a 2" x 7½" blue rectangle as shown. Make (2). Make two more which are oriented in a mirror image as shown. These are leaf units.

7. Sew a 2" x 1½" blue rectangle to the bottom edge of the first leaf units. Sew a 2" x 2½" blue rectangle to the bottom edge of the mirror image leaf units. (See both in the diagrams for steps 8 and 9.)

8. Sew a ⅞" x 2½" green piece to the short side of a 3⅛" x 2½" blue rectangle. Make (2). Sew this unit to the bottom edge of a flower unit from step #4 to create the stem. Sew a leaf unit from step #7 (the shorter ones) to the side of a flower/stem unit, as shown in the diagram. Make (2). (Mirror image units will be used in the next step.) These Flower Sections should measure 5" x 8½".

9. For the mirror image flower units, the stem is longer. Sew a ⅞" x 4½" green piece to the long side of a 3⅛" x 4½" blue rectangle. Make (2). Sew this unit to the bottom edge of a mirror image flower unit from step #5 to create the stem. Sew a mirror image leaf unit (the longer ones) to the side of the mirror image flower/stem unit, as shown below, matching up the bottom edge. Make (2). This section is uneven and needs to be trimmed. Measure from the bottom edge and trim top off to make the section 8 ½" tall. Make (2) of the mirror image flower sections. They should measure 5" x 8½". You have now completed four Flower Sections.

Trim

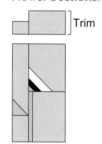

Construction for Upright Bloom Sections:

10. Sew a 3⅞" x ¾" black piece to the 3⅞" x 1½" white rectangle along the long edges. Add the 3⅞" x ¾" green piece to the black edge of the rectangle. Press all seams toward the white. Make (3).

11. Draw a diagonal line from corner to corner on the back of the (6) 2" blue squares. Use the 2" blue squares to sew corner triangles on two of the rectangle corners from step 10 as shown. Sew one, then trim and press open. Sew the second one, trim and press. Make (3).

12. Sew a 3⅞" x 4" blue rectangle onto the white edge of the piece from step 11. Make (3).

13. Place a 2" x 2¼" blue rectangle with the longest side horizontally on the table in front of you. Place a green 2" x 3½" rectangle on top of the blue rectangle vertically, with right sides together, aligning the corners. The shortest side of the green rectangle will be along the long side of the blue rectangle as shown in the diagram below. Sew in a diagonal seam across the corner from the corner of the blue piece on the bottom to the corner of the green piece on top. You can draw a line to sew on if you need it as a guide. Trim the seam allowance to ¼" and press open. This is a diagonal seam.

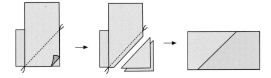

14. Use the joined piece from step 13 as the bottom piece, and sew another diagonal seam (in the same direction) with the blue 2" x 4¾" rectangle on top. Trim seam allowance to ¼" and press open. Make (3) of these units.

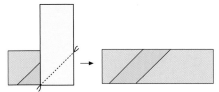

15. Sew a ⅞" x 6½" green piece to the long side of the unit from step 14 as shown. Press toward the green. Make (3).

16. Join a blue 2" x 3¼" rectangle and a green 2" x 3½" rectangle in a diagonal seam, with the pieces oriented as shown in diagram. Trim and press. Make (3).

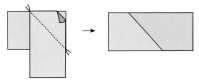

17. Sew a blue 2" x 3¾" rectangle to the piece from step 16 in a diagonal seam orienting as shown. Trim and press. Make (3). (These are the right side of stem/leaf unit.) Sew each to the green side of a unit from step 15 to create a stem/leaf unit.

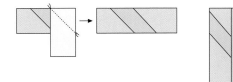

18. Sew a stem/leaf unit from step 17 to the bottom of the bloom unit from step 12 as shown. Make (3).

19. Your sections need to be trimmed to center the flowers at different heights. Trim one section to 8½" in height by measuring from the top edge. Trim the second section by measuring from the bottom edge to 8½" in height. Trim the third section by measuring from the top of the white flower down the stem and cut off at 6½". Then measure from this bottom edge to 8½" in height and trim off top. All the blocks should now measure 3⅞" x 8½". (These trimming directions are approximate. The point here is to have the same flower at different heights. Just make sure your sections end up 8½" tall.) You have completed 3 Upright Bloom Sections.

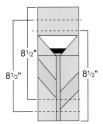

Construction for Branching Bloom Section:

20. Sew a green ⅞" x 2½" piece to the left side of the white 1¼" x 2½". Press toward green.

21. Draw a diagonal line from corner to corner on the back of the two 1½" blue squares. Sew these squares on to the rectangle from step 20 in corner triangles as shown. This little flower will face right.

22. Sew a blue rectangle 1½" x 1" to the bottom of flower from step 21. Sew a 1⅝" x 3" blue rectangle to the right side of these pieces. Last, sew a 2⅝" x 1¾" blue rectangle to the top of these pieces, along the long edge. Follow the diagram.

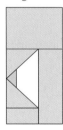

23. To a blue 2" x 2¼" rectangle, sew a corner triangle using a green 2" square, as shown. Add a 1⅛" x 2¼" rectangle to the right side.

24. Sew the unit from step 23 to the top of the unit from step 22. Sew a green ⅞" x 6" strip to the left side as shown.

25. Join a blue 1½" x 3⅝" blue rectangle with a diagonal seam to a 1⅞" x 1½" green rectangle.

Trim and press, then join a blue 1½" x 3½" rectangle in a diagonal seam going the same direction as shown.

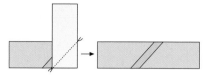

26. Make another unit like the one in step 25, except that the blue rectangles are not as long: Use a blue 1½" x 2½" diagonally seamed (the same direction) to a 1⅞" x 1½" green in the first step, then add a blue 1½" x 2⅝". The finished piece will be 4" long. Sew a green 1½"corner triangle on the left side as shown.

27. Sew the unit made in step 25 to the left (green) side of the unit from step 24. Sew the unit from step 26 to the top of these joined units.

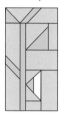

28. Draw a diagonal line from corner to corner on a white 2" square. Place the square on top of a 2" blue square. Sew on the diagonal line to make a corner triangle. Trim seam allowance and press. Place the 1" green square on the white corner and sew in a corner triangle. Trim and press. Sew this unit to the short side of the remaining blue rectangle, 2½" x 2" as shown.

29. Sew the unit from step 28 to the top edge of the unit from step 27 as shown.

30. Sew a white 2½" square in a corner triangle on the bottom edge of a 2½" s 5½" blue rectangle. On that same corner, sew a 1½" black square in a corner triangle. Finally, add a green corner triangle using a 1" square on the same corner as shown. Sew a blue 2½" x 3½" rectangle below the flower making a long strip.

31. Add the strip from step 30 to the side of the unit from step 29. This is your completed Branching Bloom Section. (Thank goodness there is only **one** of these!) Your finished section should measure 6" x 8 ½".

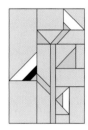

Let's Sew the Block Together:

32. Follow the diagram below to put the block together. Use the spacer pieces as listed in the cutting directions.

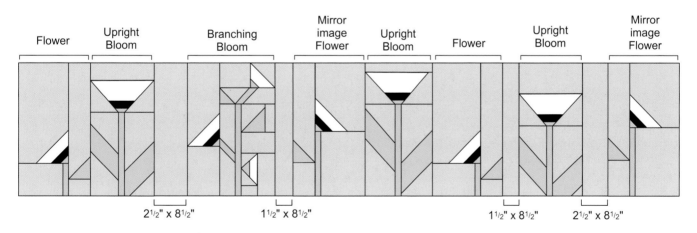

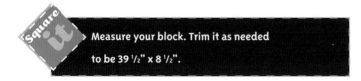

Measure your block. Trim it as needed to be 39 ½" x 8 ½".

Wildflower Melody

SETTING THE QUILT TOGETHER

Cutting:

From Black: (13) strips, 2" x width of fabric, cut and piece as needed to make: (6) 2" x 12½", (6) 2" x 39½", (2) 2" x 61½", (8) strips, 3½" x width of fabric, cut and piece as needed to make: (2) 3½" x 56½", (2) 3½" x 81½"

From Cream print: (6) strips, 5 ½" x width of fabric, cut and piece to make: (2) 5½" x 42½", (2) 5½" x 71½"

From Green: (7) strips, 1¼" x with of fabric, cut and piece to make: (2) 1¼" x 52½", (2) 1¼" x 73"

From Light Blue: (7) strips, 2½" x width of fabric, cut and piece to make: (2) 2½" x 52½", (2) 2½" x 75½"

Construction:

(See: A Note About Borders on page 14.)

1. Lay out blocks as shown. Sew each row of the quilt center together with black 2" x 12½" sashing between blocks 1 and 2; 2 and 3; 4 and 5; 5 and 6; 7 and 8; 8 and 9.

Block 10		
Block 1	Block 2	Block 3
Block 4	Block 5	Block 6
Block 7	Block 8	Block 9
Block 11		

2. Sew a black 2" x 39½" sashing strip on the top of each row. Sew the rows together. Sew one more strip on the bottom of the last row.

3. Sew Block 10 above the center section of the quilt. Sew Block 11 below the quilt center.

4. Sew the last two black 2" x 39½" sashing strips to the top and bottom of quilt.

5. Sew the black 2" x 61½" sashing strips to the sides of the quilt.

ADD BORDERS:

Refer to photo on page 83.

6. Sew a Cream print 5½" x 42½" border on the top and bottom of the quilt. Sew a Cream print 5½" x 71½" border on the sides of the quilt.

7. Take the 1¼" wide Green strips to the ironing board. Press in half lengthwise wrong sides together to create a flat piping.

8. Place the 52½" green piping and the light blue border of the same length together with the long raw edges even. Place on the top and bottom edges of the quilt with the right sides together and raw edges even. The green piping strip will be sandwiched between the quilt and the border. Sew using a ¼" seam as usual. Press the light blue border open with the green piping laying on top of the cream print.

9. Fold under the end of a green 73" piping strip 45 degrees so that the raw edges are even.

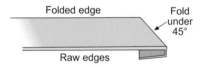

10. Place along the right side edge of the quilt with this folded edge even with the green piping in the top border. Align the long raw edges. Baste in place. When you get close to the lower edge of the quilt, fold the end of the green piping 45 degrees as you did the top, to end even with the green piping in the lower border. Repeat for other side.

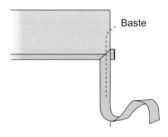

11. Place the 75½" light blue borders right sides together on the sides of the quilt. The green piping will be sandwiched between quilt and borders. Stitch in place. Press the light blue borders open, with the green piping laying on the cream print.

12. Sew the black 3½" x 56½" borders to the top and bottom of the quilt.

13. Sew the black 3½" x 81½" borders to the sides of the quilt. Your quilt top is done! Layer with batting and backing, quilt and bind.

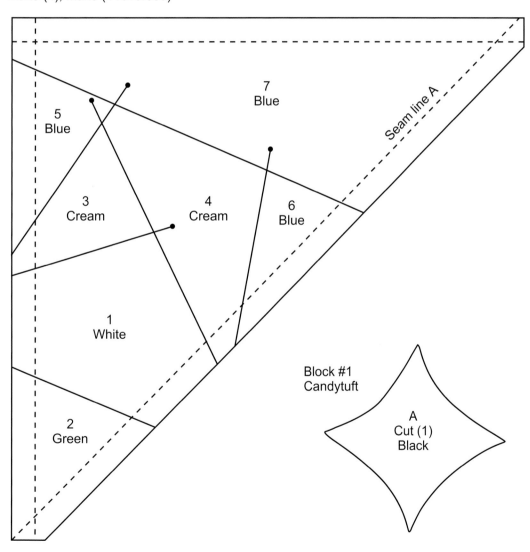

Block #1 Candytuft
Main Foundation Pattern
Make (4), Make (4 reversed)

7
Blue

Seam line A

5
Blue

3
Cream

4
Cream

6
Blue

1
White

Block #1
Candytuft

A
Cut (1)
Black

2
Green

Wildflower Melody

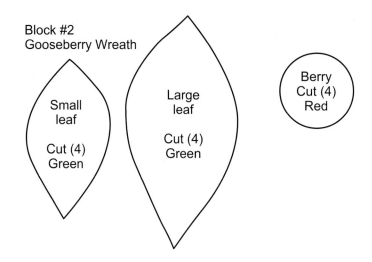

Block #2
Gooseberry Wreath

Small
leaf

Cut (4)
Green

Large
leaf

Cut (4)
Green

Berry
Cut (4)
Red

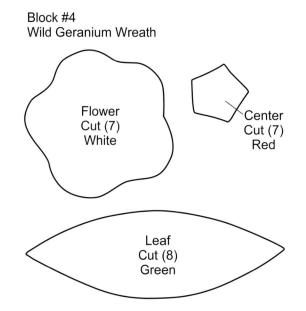

Block #4
Wild Geranium Wreath

Flower
Cut (7)
White

Center
Cut (7)
Red

Leaf
Cut (8)
Green

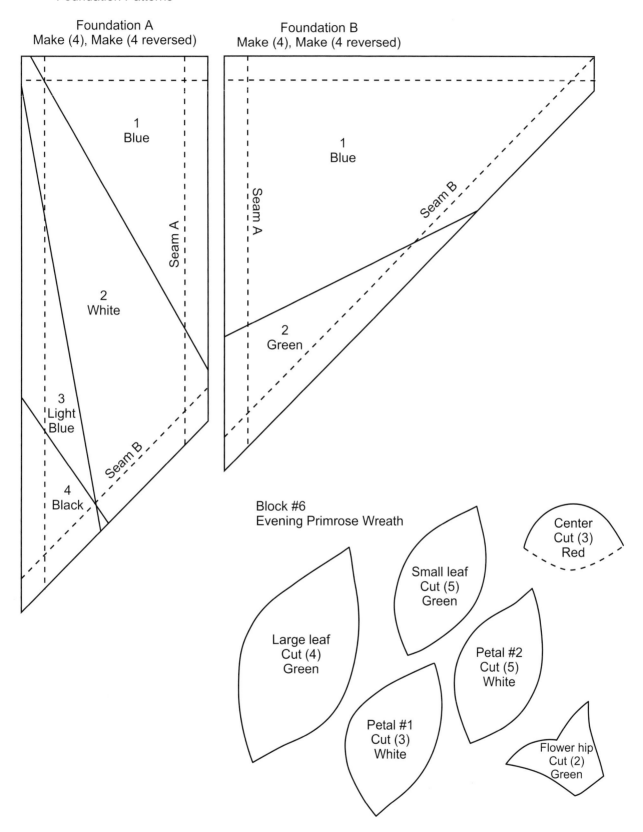

Block #5 Sego Lily
Foundation Patterns

Foundation A
Make (4), Make (4 reversed)

1
Blue

Seam A

2
White

3
Light
Blue

Seam B

4
Black

Foundation B
Make (4), Make (4 reversed)

Seam A

1
Blue

Seam B

2
Green

Block #6
Evening Primrose Wreath

Center
Cut (3)
Red

Small leaf
Cut (5)
Green

Large leaf
Cut (4)
Green

Petal #2
Cut (5)
White

Petal #1
Cut (3)
White

Flower hip
Cut (2)
Green

Wildflower Melody

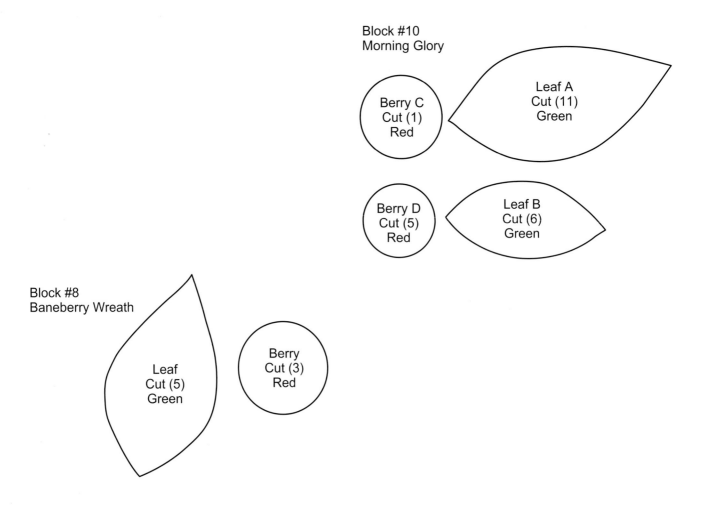

Block #10
Morning Glory

Berry C
Cut (1)
Red

Leaf A
Cut (11)
Green

Berry D
Cut (5)
Red

Leaf B
Cut (6)
Green

Block #8
Baneberry Wreath

Leaf
Cut (5)
Green

Berry
Cut (3)
Red

Placement Diagram Block #10 "Wildflower Melody"

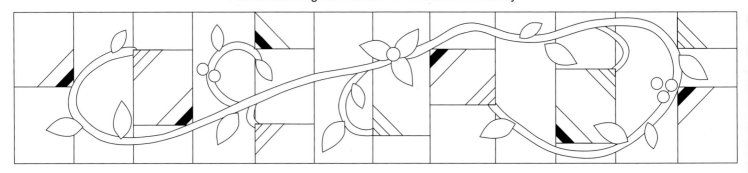

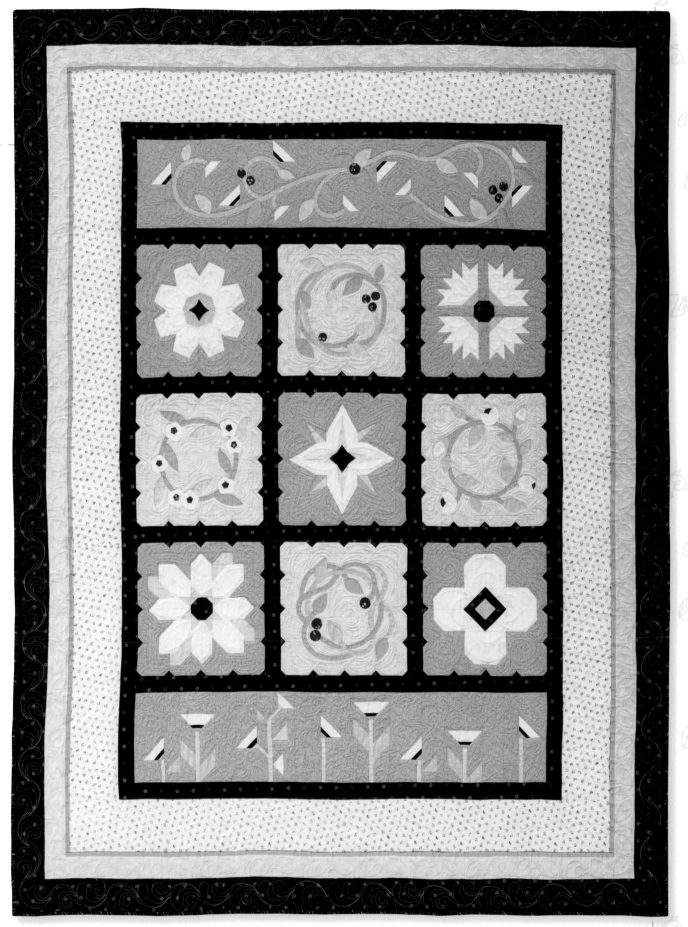

Wildflower Melody, 2009. 62" x 81" Pieced and appliquéd by Jill Finley; quilted by Virginia Gore.

"You know it's time for Quilt Retreat when..."

...your family says things like, 'remember the time when Mom used to cook?'"

...you can't find the floor in the sewing room."

...you start counting down with childlike glee, and Christmas, for everyone else, was months ago."

...there are plastic bins stacked up everywhere!"

...when you have to add 'make a quilt' to your homework list."

...you've packed more chocolate than clothes!"

...you've spent more money on fabric and quilt supplies in the last month than you've spent at the grocery store!

...the dishes are piled in the sink, the laundry's piled in the hall, and you and your favorite sisters are piled in the car."

...your husband is wearing his 'I'm-trying-to-be-patient' look almost all the time now."

...your sewing machine is finally getting its much needed tune-up/service so it can sew another 900 hrs in just a few days."

...everything in the refrigerator and freezer is labeled **Do Not Eat—For Quilt Retreat Only.**"

...your husband starts asking you (in a slightly panicked kind of voice), 'Now **when** are you leaving?' and 'Now when will you be **back**?' and '**Where** did all these kids come from?'"

...it feels like forever since you've had a really good laugh, a really good cry, and really good conversation."

All Together Now Salad

Tori brought this yummy salad a few years ago, and it was a hit. Add some crunchy breadsticks and you will be back to sewing in no time.

Tori's All Together Now Salad
1 large bundle spinach, washed and torn (or a 12 oz. bag)
1 bunch green onion, chopped
1 large yellow bell pepper, thinly sliced
1 large red bell pepper, thinly sliced
1 - 16 oz. package large egg noodles, cooked and cooled
4-6 chicken breasts cooked and cut into bite size pieces

Dressing:
$^1/_4$ cup sesame seeds (1 oz container)
3 T parsley flakes
$^1/_2$ cup red wine vinegar
$^1/_2$ cup soy sauce
$^1/_2$ cup vegetable oil
1 clove minced garlic
$^1/_2$ teaspoons Ground ginger
$^1/_3$ cup sugar
$^1/_4$ teaspoons pepper
$^1/_4$ teaspoons salt

Topping:
1 cup sliced almonds
3 tablespoons butter
$^1/_2$ cup brown sugar

For topping, place all ingredients in frying pan until butter is melted and almonds are coated. Lay the almonds out on wax paper to let dry.

Place noodles and chicken in a large bowl. Pour half of the dressing over. Let stand for at least 10 minutes. Mix in greens and vegetables, add remaining dressing and sprinkle with nuts. Enjoy! Serves 8-10 quilters.

Hugs and Kisses

FINISHED SIZE: 43" x 49"

This is a good quilt to make in teams. Team X will make the (15) "X" Blocks for each quilter. Team O will make (15) "O" Blocks for each quilter. Each quilter will set her own blocks together. One person can bring all the fabrics, or you can have each quilter bring a few of each color. Either way, it will be easiest to use all the same background.

CUTTING INSTRUCTIONS

Team "X"
Assorted Browns: (7) sets of (4) 3" x 3"
Assorted Blues: (8) sets of (4) 3" x 3"
White background: (120) 1½" x 1½"

Team "O"
Assorted Pinks: (15) sets of (2) 5½" x 2½" and (2) 2½" x 1½"
White background: (15) 1½" x 1½", (60) 2" x 2"

Each quilter
White background: (25) 5½" x 1½", (6) 35½" x 1½", (2) 31½" x 1½"
Blue border: (4) 37½" x 3½"
Bright Pink border: (2) 43½" x 1½", (2) 39½" x 1½"
Light Pink border: (2) 43½" x 2½", (2) 45½" x 2½"

See "A Note About Borders" on page 14.

SEWING INSTRUCTIONS

"X" Blocks

1. Draw a diagonal line on the back of (120) 1½" white squares from corner to corner.

2. Place a white 1½" square on a blue 3" square right sides together, with corners matching and drawn line going across the corner.

3. Sew on the drawn line. Trim away leaving a ¼" seam allowance. Press open with seam allowance toward the white.

4. Repeat for opposite corner, trimming and pressing toward the blue.

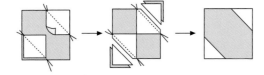

FABRIC REQUIREMENTS
1 yard White background
¼ yard total assorted Blues
¼ yard total assorted Browns
½ yard total assorted Pinks
½ yard Blue for border
¼ yard Bright Pink for border
½ yard Light Pink for border
½ yard Brown Check
   for binding
2 ⅝ yards Backing
   (with just one seam)

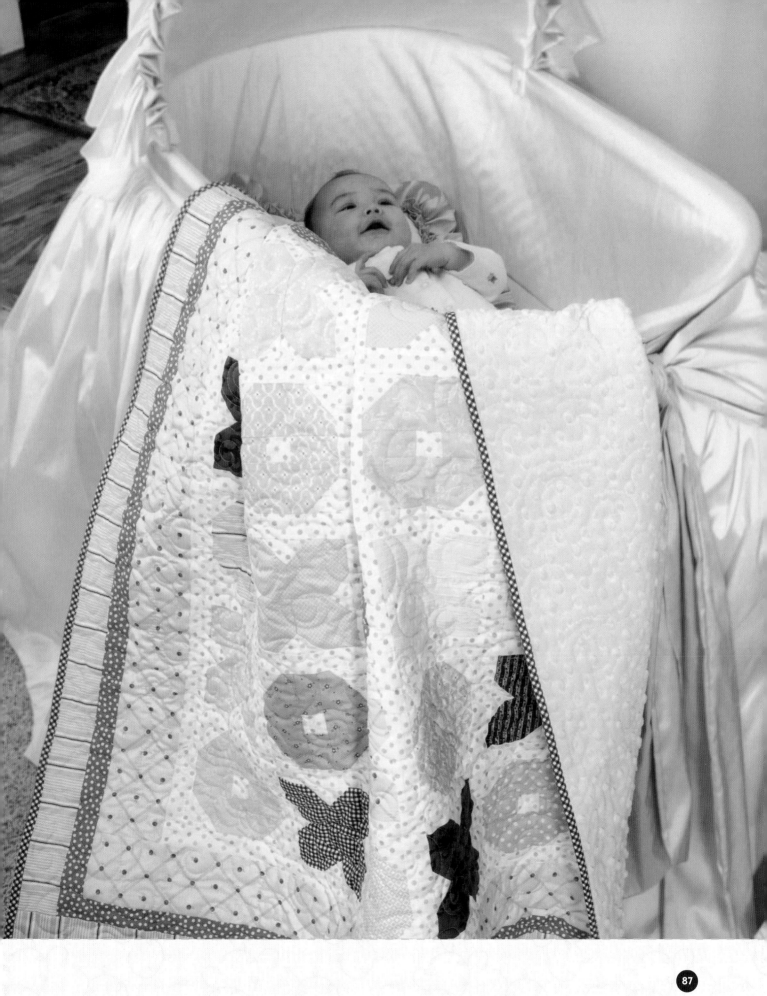

5. Sew white corner triangles on each blue 3" square. Put four 3" blue squares together four-patch fashion, with 2 in each row, and then sew the rows together to make the "X". Make a total of (15) "X" blocks for each quilt, (8) blue, and (7) brown.

"O" Blocks

1. Draw a diagonal line on the back of the (60) 2" white squares, from corner to corner.

2. Place a white 2" square right sides together with a pink 2½" x 5½" rectangle. Match up the corners with the drawn line going across the corner.

3. Sew on the drawn line. Trim leaving a ¼" seam allowance. Press toward the pink. Sew a second white corner triangle on the adjacent corner on the long side.

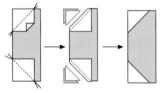

4. Sew white corner triangles on each pink 2½" x 5½" piece.

5. Sew a white 1½" square between two 1½" x 2 ½" pink pieces (in a set) along the short sides.

6. Sew the pink pieces in a set together with the 1½" strip in the middle and the white corner triangles on the outside.

7. Make (15) pink "O" blocks for each quilt.

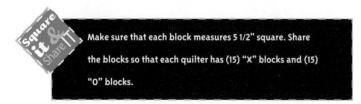

Make sure that each block measures 5 1/2" square. Share the blocks so that each quilter has (15) "X" blocks and (15) "O" blocks.

Setting the Quilt Together

1. Lay out the blocks according to quilt diagram. Alternate the X's and O's with 5 blocks across and 6 blocks down.

2. Sew a 1½" x 5½" white strip between all the blocks in each column.

3. Sew the 1½" x 35½" white strips between the columns and on the outside of the quilt center.

4. Sew the 1½" x 31½" white strips to the top and bottom of the quilt center.

5. Sew (2) 37½" x 3½" blue strips to the sides of the quilt center. Sew the other (2) 37½" x 3 ½" blue strips to the top and bottom.

6. Sew the 43½" bright pink strips to the sides of the quilt. Sew the bright pink 39½" strips to the top and bottom of the quilt.

7. Sew the light pink 45½" x 2½" strips to the sides of quilt. Sew the light pink 43½" x 2½" strips to the top and bottom of quilt.

8. The quilt top is done! I layered it with batting and used a "minky" fabric for the backing. Quilt as desired and bind. You have a soft and cute baby quilt!

Assembly Diagram

Hugs and Kisses, 2009. 43" x 49" Pieced by Jill Finley;
quilted by Peggy Shadel.

Just For Fun

Sometimes it is fun to work on the same project but do all your own work. These little projects are perfect for the simple classes you might offer for individuals. You can teach a new technique along with each project, such as embroidery or working with ric rac.

These projects are also good for a retreat because they are quick and fun and a nice break from traditional piecing. Each quilter can go home with something actually **finished**. That brings satisfaction and a positive vibe to the rest of the event. Happy quilters with finished projects add to a successful retreat.

At our retreat, the only limiting factor on these fun little classes is finding space to teach all the requested projects!

Fresh Baked

This simple and quick pin cushion looks good enough to eat! Change the colors to make a raspberry or cinnamon roll.

CUTTING INSTRUCTIONS
Orange fabric: (1) strip 3½" x 23", (1) pattern A
Cream fabric: (1) strip 3½" x 23"
Green fabric: (1) pattern A reversed

SEWING INSTRUCTIONS

1. Place the 3½" x 23" strips of orange and cream right sides together. Sew along one long edge, turn and sew across the short edge and down the other long side. Use a ¼" seam. Leave one short side open.

2. Turn right side out and press.

3. Stuff tube gently with polyester stuffing, keeping it about 1" thick and flat. I like to put a little sand or crushed walnuts in the bottom edge of the tube to add a little weight at the bottom. To do this, slide a narrow ruler in the tube between the stuffing and the bottom seam. Pour, or spoon, the sand in slowly as you move the ruler up all along the long edge of the bottom seam toward the opening.

4. Turn in the edges of the opening and sew closed.

5. Starting at one short end, gently roll up the tube with the orange fabric on the inside. Secure the end in place with pins, then stitch by hand to keep the roll rolled up.

6. Stitch the roll together by hand on the bottom side. Start in the center and spiral out. This won't show, but will stabilize the pin cushion.

7. Make the "wrapper" by placing the piece "A" of orange and "A" reversed of green right sides together. Stitch all around the outside edge in a ¼" seam. Cut a 2" X in the center of the orange side only. Turn the right side out and press. The cut will not show, it will be on the inside of the pin cushion.

FABRIC AND SUPPLY REQUIREMENTS
⅓ yard Orange fabric
⅛ yard Cream fabric
10" x 10" Green fabric
White or Clear seed beads
Orange bugle beads
1 yard Orange or Green ribbon, ⅜" wide
Polyester stuffing
1 cup Sand or Crushed Walnuts (optional)

Fresh Baked, 2009. Pieced by Jill Finley.

Fresh Baked

SOFT AND SWEET ORANGE ROLLS

My mom was an amazing cook...an amazing woman for that matter. She taught her five daughters the joy of creating a beautiful home, full of love and learning and sweet smells from the kitchen. She taught us to sew and cook and clean and work hard and enjoy life. This is her recipe for rolls, and I make them into Orange Rolls by adding a little more sugar and more butter, two of my favorite ingredients. And of course, the oranges. Yum! You can make the dough up to 5 days ahead. Then get them out of the fridge and roll them out at the retreat to make fresh hot orange rolls.

Mom's Soft and Sweet Orange Rolls

2 tablespoons Yeast, dissolved in ¹/₂ cup warm water
3 eggs
¹/₂ cup Sugar
¹/₄ cup Butter
1 cup Milk, warmed
5 cup Flour
2 teaspoons Salt

Dissolve yeast, set aside. Whip eggs and add sugar. Melt butter and add to warmed milk. Combine flour and salt and add to egg mixture a little at a time alternated with the milk and butter. Add yeast after half of the flour is incorporated. This will make a soft dough. You can add a little more flour if the dough is too sticky. Knead for a few minutes. Place the dough into a large oiled bowl. Cover loosely with plastic wrap. Let the dough raise to double in size. Punch down. Refrigerate covered overnight or until chilled.

Filling:
¹/₂ cup butter
zest of 2 large oranges
¹/₃ cup sugar

Melt butter and add orange zest. Set aside. Roll out cooled dough to a rectangle about 12" x 20" and ³/₈" thick. Brush dough with orange butter and sprinkle the sugar on top. Roll up the rectangle from the long edge. With a sharp knife or using a thread, cut into 1 ¹/₂" slices. Place cut side down on greased cookie sheet. Cover with greased plastic wrap, let rise until double in size. Bake at 375° for about 15 minutes until light golden brown. Remove from oven and brush with melted butter. Cool for 15 minutes. Spread with icing.

Icing:
2 cups powdered sugar
3 tablespoons orange juice (squeeze from zested oranges)
3-4 tablespoons heavy cream

8. Place the "wrapper" with the orange side up. Place the orange roll in the center of the "wrapper." Gather the edges of the "wrapper" up around the sides of the orange roll. Wrap the ribbon around the "wrapper" to hold it in place. Tie in a bow.

9. Adjust the gathers in the "wrapper."

10. Embellish the top of your orange roll with white seed beads (sugar) and orange bugle beads (zest). Sew randomly in place individually by hand. Travel from one spot to the next inside the roll so your stitches don't show.

11. Add a few pins and enjoy!

Place powdered sugar in mixing bowl with orange juice and 2 tablespoons of cream. Beat until smooth. Add more cream as needed to get the desired consistency. Makes about 20-24 rolls.

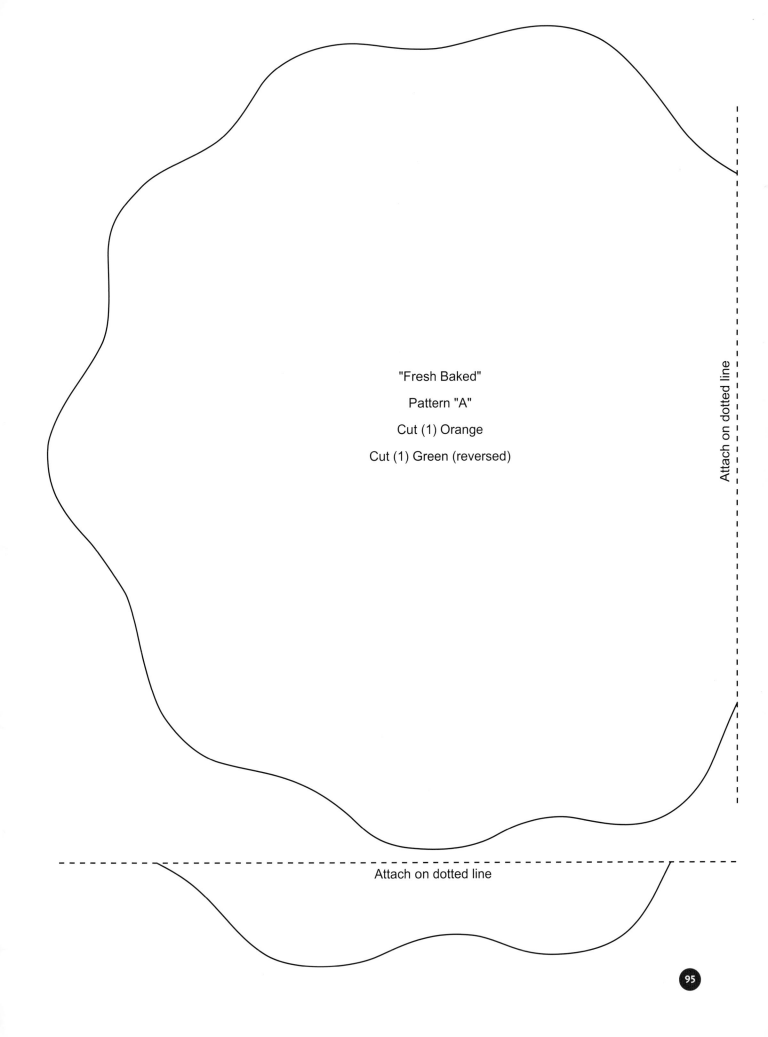

"Fresh Baked"

Pattern "A"

Cut (1) Orange

Cut (1) Green (reversed)

Attach on dotted line

Attach on dotted line

Fresh Squeezed

These little pin cushions will give your sewing space the zest it needs! I have given you templates for two sizes, a grapefruit, and an orange. You can make a whole collection of citrus!

CUTTING INSTRUCTIONS

From cotton quilting fabric: (8) template Side A , (1) template Top B from cream

From felt or felted wool: (Do not add seam allowances to wool pieces. Cut on the line, edges will not be turned.) (8) template Section C from pink or orange, (1) template Edging E from peach or light pink, (2 for orange and 3 for grapefruit) template Seed D from peach or light pink

CONSTRUCTION

1. Place two of pattern piece A right sides together with edges even. Stitch along one long curved side with a ¼" seam. Open up and press seam to one side. Make three more pairs of piece "A" for a total of four.

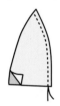

2. Place 2 pairs of A right sides together matching and nesting seams together. Stitch on one long curved side. Press seam to one side. Make one more. These units are one half of the citrus bottom.

3. Place the two halves together, matching seams and edges, nesting seams together. Sew the curved sides together with a ¼" seam. Press. This is the citrus bottom.

FABRIC AND SUPPLY REQUIREMENTS

Total of ⅛ yd of Yellow or Orange quilting cotton (Choose colors based on which fruit you are making. I used 4 different yellows for the grapefruit, and 4 different oranges for the orange.)

6" x 6" piece of Cream quilting cotton

6" x 6" piece of Pink or Orange felt or felted wool

6" x 6" piece of Cream felt or felted wool

Embroidery floss (pink or orange and peach)

Polyester stuffing

Coarse salt, sand or ground shells for weight. (optional)

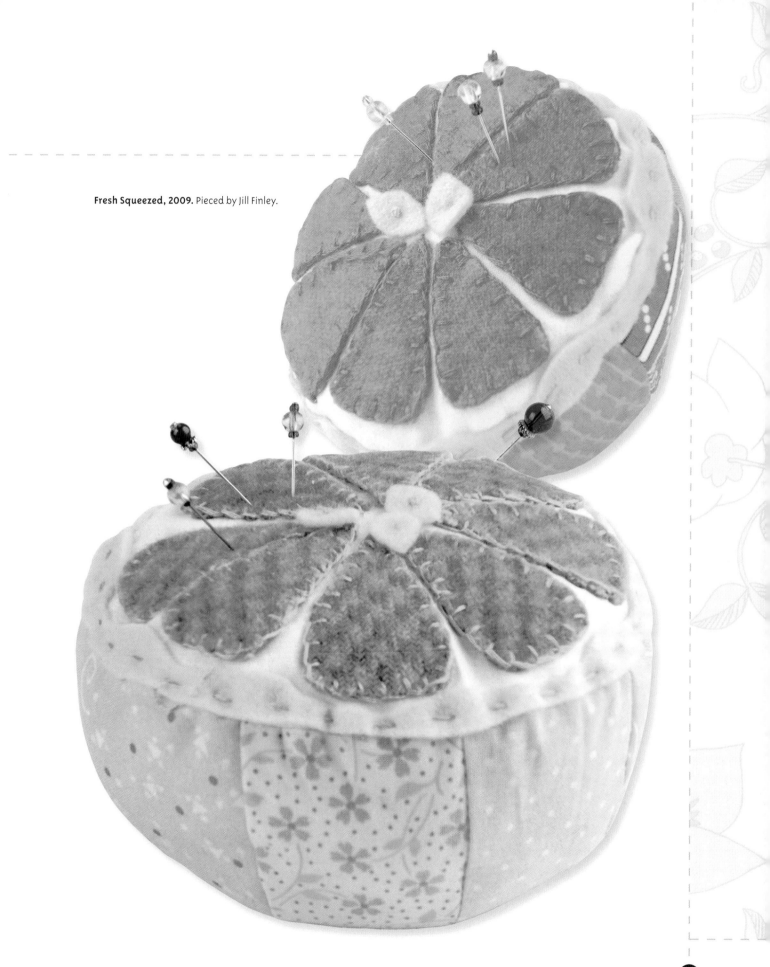

Fresh Squeezed, 2009. Pieced by Jill Finley.

Fresh Squeezed

4. Take piece B, fold circle in half and then in quarters and press lightly to create placement lines. Fold one more time to divide circle into eight sections. Press.

5. Place a piece C on the round top piece into each marked section. Baste in place with a few drops of Jillily Studio Appli-Glue.

6. Stitch around each of piece C in a blanket stitch, using two strands of embroidery floss.

7. Place (2) for Orange or (3) for Grapefruit of piece D (Seeds) randomly in the center of the circle top. Stitch each in place with one French knot using embroidery floss.

8. Place piece B (Top) right side up with the Citrus bottom from Step #3 on top with the right sides together and matching the outside raw edge. Beginning at one section seam, stitch around edge using a ¼" seam. Leave one section open to turn right side out. Turn.

9. Stuff with polyester stuffing (it is the easiest for pins to go through), keeping the shape of the top flat and the bottom section round. After you are happy with the arrangement of the stuffing, I like to add a little sand, or coarse salt, or ground shells in the very bottom to add weight and make the pin cushion "sit." Just spoon it in around the stuffing. Hand stitch opening closed.

10. Place piece E (felt edging) on top covering the outside seam. Stitch in place with embroidery floss using a running stitch. This adds some fun texture and detail. Enjoy!

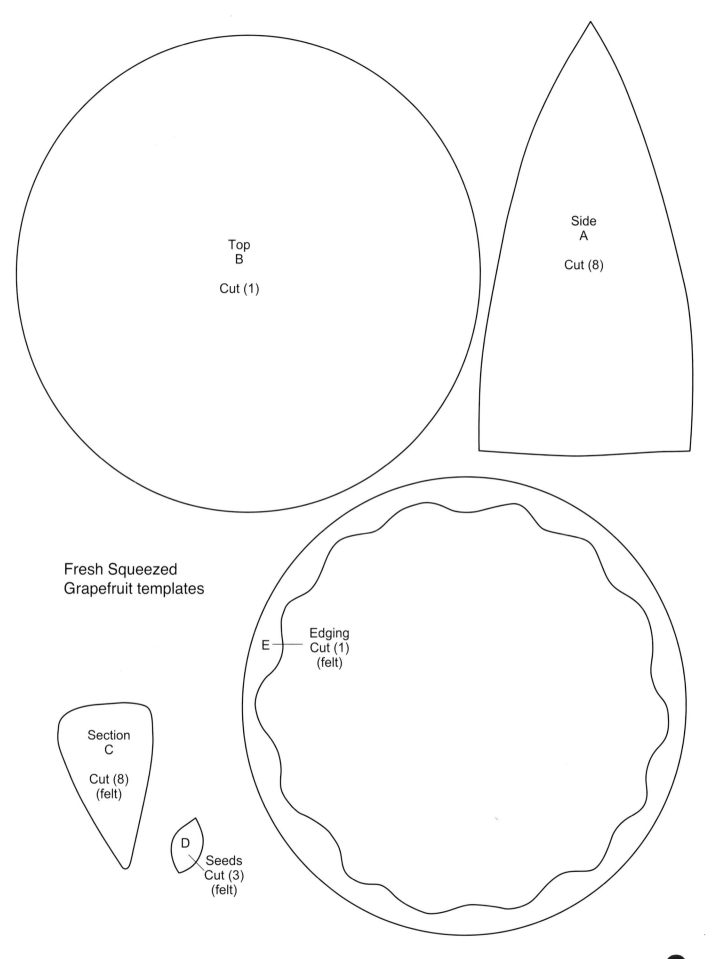

Top
B

Cut (1)

Side
A

Cut (8)

Fresh Squeezed
Grapefruit templates

E — Edging
Cut (1)
(felt)

Section
C

Cut (8)
(felt)

D
Seeds
Cut (3)
(felt)

Fresh Squeezed

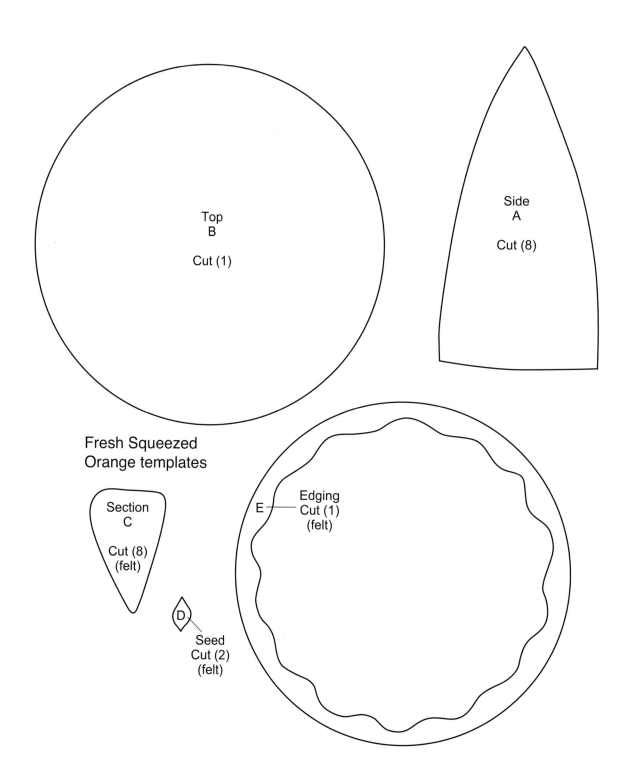

Top
B

Cut (1)

Side
A

Cut (8)

Fresh Squeezed
Orange templates

Section
C

Cut (8)
(felt)

D
Seed
Cut (2)
(felt)

E — Edging
Cut (1)
(felt)

Overheard at Quilt Retreat

Melissa: "No quilter left behind."

Becky: "We should not be rewarding slackers."

April: "I have psychic bobbin abilities."

Amy B.: "I'm doing the work of 10 men."

Karen: "We're not halfway done. **Sarah:** "We're halfway done with half of them!"

Jenn: "Some people say it out loud, and some people throw things."

Jane: "I know I learned something new this year, but I can't remember what it is."

Sarah: "I'm not even going to pretend I know what's going on."

Jenn: "We don't need perfect, we just need done."

Lacey: "I just did something bad. Does it matter?"

Emily: "You're fired!" **Jane:** "Okay!"

GG (great-grandma): "You are a quilting marvel."

Jann: "Just pretend it's right."

Tori: "It's better that one block should dwindle than the whole quilt should lose its points."

GG: "But if I sit on a pillow, my legs can't reach the pedal."

Sunny Side Up

This is a reversible apron, just perfect for putting dinner on and doing a little sewing after! (Or vise versa.) Use several different fabrics to add a little more interest. I used two different fabrics on each side. One for the apron body and one for the neck straps, ruffle, and pocket. On the other side I used two more.

CUTTING INSTRUCTIONS

From Fabrics 1 and 3: (1) apron body
From Fabrics 2 and 4: (2) ties, 2½" x 31", (1) ruffle on fold, (2) neck straps (with the fabric wrong sides together so you get one and a mirror image), (1) pocket on fold

Cutting Apron Body:

Cut a rectangle 30" x 23". Fold in half resulting in a 15" x 23" rectangle. Place Template A on one raw edged corner, and Template B on the adjacent raw edged corner as show below. Cut away through both layers leaving your apron body. The fold will be down the center of the apron.

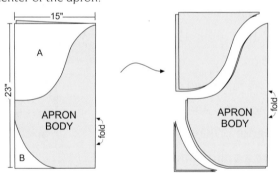 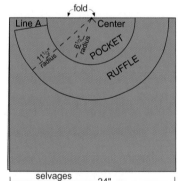

Cutting Pocket and Ruffle:

Cut a width of fabric to 24". Measure along the fold edge to mark the center at 12" from cut edge. Use a compass to mark an arc with a radius of 6½". You can use a chalk pencil, or a regular pencil to draw the line. (If you do not have a compass, you can use a ruler or string.) This inside arc outlines the Pocket. Use your compass again and mark a second arc with a radius of 11½". This arc outlines the Ruffle. Cut out the pocket and the ruffle through 2 layers with the fold intact. The ruffle does not extend all the way from fold to fold. It ends approximately 2" from the fold. Cut off as indicated on Line A.

SEWING INSTRUCTIONS

1. Turn the round edge of the folded pockets under ¼" with your iron. You can use a freezer paper pattern if you like to press the seam edge over.

Sunny Side Up, 2009. Pieced by Margaret Brockbank.

2. Center the pocket on the apron body, 1½" up from the bottom edge of apron body. Top stitch in place around the round edge. Sew a straight line down the center of the pocket to divide it into two pockets. Make one apron body each of fabric 1 and fabric 3.

3. Place a fabric 2 ruffle and a fabric 4 ruffle right sides together and stitch in a ¼" seam along a short end, and all around the outside edge of the curved ruffle, and then back up the other short end. Turn to the right side and press.

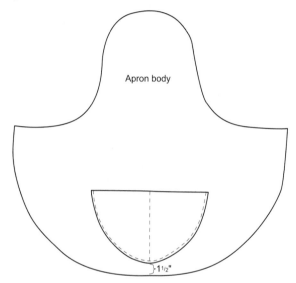

Apron body

1½"

4. Pair up a tie of fabric 2 with a tie of fabric 4, right sides together. Sew together with a ¼" seam all along the long edge and across the end diagonally and back down the other long edge. Turn to the right side and press. Make (2).

5. Sew neck strap piece C to neck strap piece D as marked on pattern. Make 4 (1 and 1 reverse of fabric 2 and fabric 4).

6. Pair up the neck straps of fabric 2 with fabric 4 right sides together. Stitch around the outside edge leaving front end open. Turn and press.

7. Place the ruffle along the bottom edge of one apron body, matching up the raw edges. Baste in place with a ¼" seam.

8. Place the raw end of the ties on one apron body as shown in diagram with raw edges even. Baste.

9. Now place the neck straps on the top of the apron bib, as shown with the raw edges even. The curve of the strap needs to match the curve of the apron bib. Baste in place.

10. Place the other apron body on top with the right sides together. Sew all around the edge of the apron encasing the ruffle, straps and ties between the two Apron Bodies **and** leaving a space about 3" wide **open** so you can turn the apron to the right side. Use a scant ⅜" seam so your basting doesn't show.

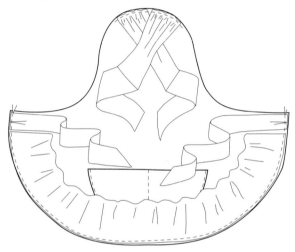

11. Turn apron right side out and press.

12. Turn seam allowance in open space, and slip stitch opening closed.

13. Overlap the ends of the neck straps with the right and left strap being at a right angle. Top stitch the edge of the square where they overlap.

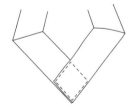

Join on dotted line

Neck Strap D

Cut (2) each fabric
with wrong sides
together

Total Cut (4)

Seam here to "D"

Neck Strap C

Cut (2) each fabric
with wrong sides
together

Total Cut (4)

Neck Strap D

Join on dotted line

(Leave front edge open)

Seam here to "C"

105

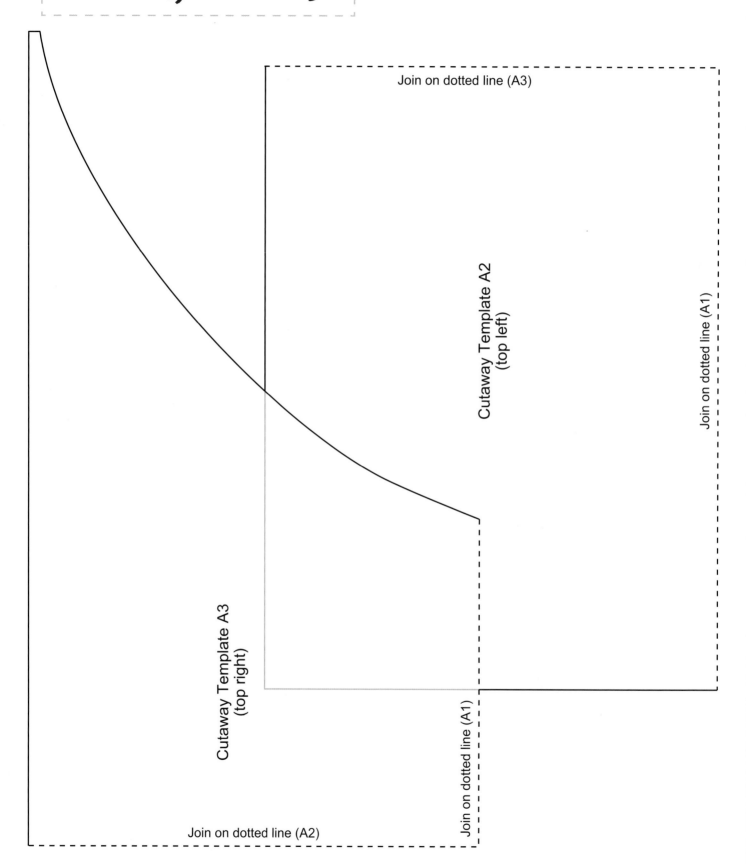

Join on dotted line (A3)

Cutaway Template A2
(top left)

Join on dotted line (A1)

Cutaway Template A3
(top right)

Join on dotted line (A1)

Join on dotted line (A2)

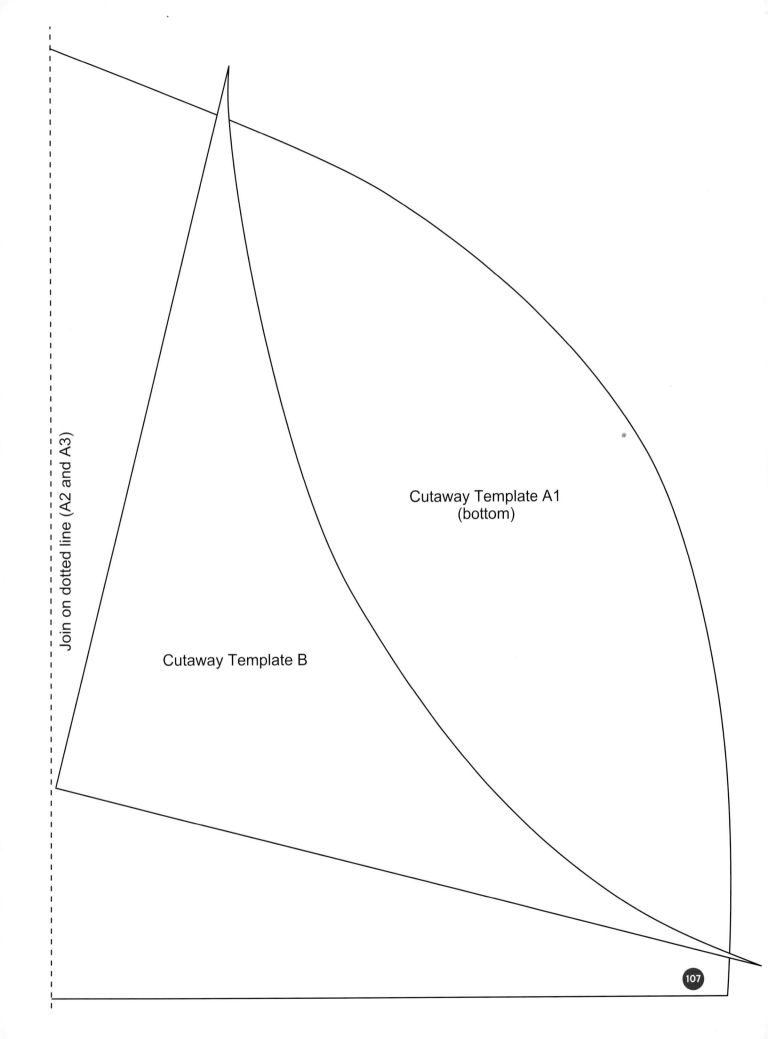

Join on dotted line (A2 and A3)

Cutaway Template A1
(bottom)

Cutaway Template B

Happy Endings

FINISHED SIZE: 5" X 7" X 1"

What a fun project! Make your own fabric from these scraps you would normally throw away, and then put them together in an irresistible little notebook cover! These little covers are fun and simple to make. Perfect for gifts, note-taking, and journaling your experiences at quilt retreat. You won't want to stop at just one!

CUTTING INSTRUCTIONS
From Backing/lining fabric: (1) 10" x 15", (2) 6½" x 7¾", (2) 2" x 4", (1) 5½" x 5½"
From Ribbon: (2) 8" pieces for ties

CONSTRUCTION
1. Overlap one selvage on top of another with the right sides up. Leave the words and color registration marks of the underneath one exposed. Show as much of the fabric as you like. Top-stitch along the bottom close to the edge to join the selvages. Repeat, adding strips of selvages until you create a piece of "selvage fabric" approximately 9" x 14".

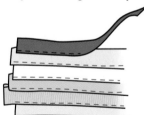

2. Layer the "selvage fabric" with the 10" x 15" batting and backing. Quilt. (I used a freehand swirly design, but you could use any pattern or follow the piecing lines.)

3. Trim the quilted cover to 7¾" x 12¼".

4. Center ric rac over seam line around the outside edge. (Seam allowance is ¼" from raw edge.) Baste in place. Place the ribbon ties at the center of each short side and baste.

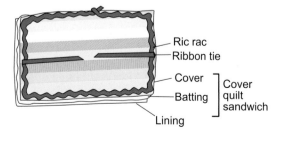

Ric rac
Ribbon tie
Cover
Batting — Cover quilt sandwich
Lining

FABRIC AND SUPPLY REQUIREMENTS
(1) 5" x 7" Spiral notebook (meaning that the pages are 5" x 7")
Selvages of 12-15 fabrics; ~1" wide by ~15" long.
1 ¼ yard ric rac
½ yard ⅜" Ribbon
⅓ yard Backing/lining fabric
10" x 15" Batting

Happy Endings, 2009. 5" x 7" x 1" Pieced by Jill Finley; quilted by Jill Finley.

Happy Endings

5. Prepare inside sleeves: Use the 6½" x 7¾" lining pieces. Hem one long side by turning under ¼" and turning again 1". Top-stitch in place. Repeat with other 6½" x 7¾" piece.

6. Prepare pocket: Hem top edge of 5½" background square by turning edge under ¼" and top-stitching. Add ribbon detail if you like. Turn under the right side of pocket ¼" and press.

7. Place pocket right side up on top of the left inside sleeve (also right side up), with the raw edges even along the left side and bottom. Top stitch on right side of pocket next to fold. Baste along bottom and remaining side.

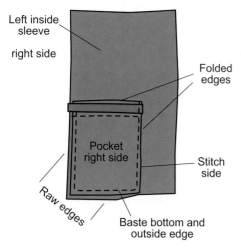

Left inside sleeve right side

Folded edges

Pocket right side

Stitch side

Raw edges

Baste bottom and outside edge

8. Prepare the spine bridge pieces: Hem one long edge of each 2" x 4" lining piece by turning under ¼" and top stitching.

9. Place the quilted cover right side up. Put the inside sleeves right side down on the quilted cover with the raw edges even on all sides. Place the spine bridge pieces along the center top and bottom edges of the quilted cover with the raw edges even. They should be right side down, and they will "bridge" the space between the inside sleeves.

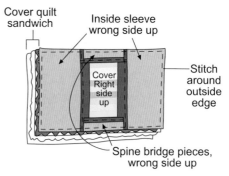

Cover quilt sandwich

Inside sleeve wrong side up

Cover Right side up

Stitch around outside edge

Spine bridge pieces, wrong side up

10. Stitch around the outside raw edge using a ¼" seam.

11. Clip corners, then turn right side out. Press firmly.

12. Insert notebook front and back covers into the inside sleeves.

Other Kansas City Star Quilts Books

Published in 2008

Portable Patchwork: Who Says You Can't Take it With You? by Donna Thomas

Quilts for Rosie: Paper Piecing Patterns from the '40s
    by Carolyn Cullinan McCormick

Fruit Salad: Appliqué Designs for Delicious Quilts by Bea Oglesby

Red, Green and Beyond by Nancy Hornback and Terry Clothier
    Thompson

A Dusty Garden Grows by Terry Clothier Thompson

We Gather Together: A Harvest of Quilts by Jan Patek

With These Hands: 19th Century-Inspired Primitive Projects for Your Home
    by Maggie Bonanomi

As the Cold Wind Blows by Barb Adams and Alma Allen

Caring for Your Quilts: Textile Conservation, Repair and Storage
    by Hallye Bone

The Circuit Rider's Quilt: An Album Quilt Honoring a Beloved Minister
    by Jenifer Dick

Embroidered Quilts: From Hands and Hearts by Christina DeArmond,
    Eula Lang and Kaye Spitzli

Reminiscing: A Whimsicals Collections by Terri Degenkolb

*Scraps and Shirttails: Reuse, Re-purpose and Recycle! The Art of Green
    Quilting* by Bonnie Hunter

Published in 2009

Flora Botanica: Quilts from the Spencer Museum of Art by Barbara Brackman

Making Memories: Simple Quilts from Cherished Clothing by Deb Rowden

Pots de Fleurs: A Garden of Appliqué Techniques by Kathy Delaney

Wedding Ring, Pickle Dish and More: Paper Piecing Curves
    by Carolyn Cullinan McCormick

The Graceful Garden: A Jacobean Fantasy Quilt by Denise Sheehan

My Stars: Patterns from The Kansas City Star, Volume I

*Opening Day: 14 Quilts Celebrating the Life and Times of Negro Leagues
    Baseball* by Sonie Ruffin

St. Louis Stars: Nine Unique Quilts that Spark by Toby Lischko

Whimsyland: Be Cre8ive with Lizzie B by Liz & Beth Hawkins

Cradle to Cradle by Barbara Jones of Quilt Soup

Pick of the Seasons: Quilts to Inspire You Through the Year by Tammy
    Johnson and Avis Shirer of Joined at the Hip

Across the Pond: Projects Inspired by Quilts of the British Isles by Bettina Havig

*Artful Bras: Hooters, Melons and Boobs, Oh My! A Quilt Guild's Fight
    Against Breast Cancer* by the Quilters of South Carolina

Flags of the American Revolution by Jan Patek

Get Your Stitch on Route 66: Quilts from the Mother Road by Christina
    DeArmond, Eula Lang and Kaye Spitzli from Of One Mind

Gone to Texas: Quilts from a Pioneer Woman's Journals by Betsy Chutchian

Juniper and Mistletoe: A Forest of Appliqué by Karla Menaugh
    and Barbara Brackman

My Stars II: Patterns from The Kansas City Star, Volume II

Nature's Offerings: Primitive Projects Inspired by the Four Seasons
    by Maggie Bonanomi

Quilts of the Golden West: Mining the History of the Gold and Silver Rush
    by Cindy Brick

Women of Influence: 12 Leaders of the Suffrage Movement by Sarah Maxwell
    and Dolores Smith

Published in 2010

Adventures with Leaders and Enders: Make More Quilts in Less Time!
    by Bonnie Hunter

A Bird in Hand: Folk Art Projects Inspired by Our Feathered Friends
    by Renee Plains

Feedsack Secrets: Fashion from Hard Times by Gloria Nixon

Greetings from Tucsadelphia: Travel-Inspired Projects from Lizzie B Cre8ive
    by Liz & Beth Hawkins

The Big Book of Bobbins: Fun, Quilty Cartoons by Julia Icenogle

Country Inn by Barb Adams and Alma Allen of Blackbird Designs

My Stars III: Patterns from The Kansas City Star, Volume III

Piecing the Past: Vintage Quilts Recreated by Kansas Troubles by Lynne
    Hagmeier

Project Books

Fan Quilt Memories by Jeanne Poore – 2000

Santa's Parade of Nursery Rhymes by Jeanne Poore – 2001

As the Crow Flies by Edie McGinnis – 2007

Sweet Inspirations by Pam Manning – 2007

Quilts Through the Camera's Eye by Terry Clothier Thompson – 2007

Louisa May Alcott: Quilts of Her Life, Her Work, Her Heart by Terry
    Clothier Thompson – 2008

The Lincoln Museum Quilt: A Reproduction for Abe's Frontier Cabin by
    Barbara Brackman and Deb Rowden – 2008

Dinosaurs – Stomp, Chomp and Roar by Pam Manning – 2008

Carrie Hall's Sampler: Favorite Blocks from a Classic Pattern Collection by
    Barbara Brackman – 2008

Just Desserts: Quick Quilts Using Pre-cut Fabrics by Edie McGinnis – 2009

Christmas at Home: Quilts for Your Holiday Traditions by Christina
    DeArmond, Eula Lang and Kaye Spitzli – 2009

Geese in the Rose Garden by Dawn Heese – 2009

Winter Trees by Jane Kennedy – 2009

Ruby Red Dots: Fanciful Circle-Inspired Designs by Sheri M. Howard – 2009

Backyard Blooms by Barbara Jones – 2010

*Not Your Grandmother's Quilt: An Appliqué Twist on Traditional Pieced
    Blocks* by Sheri M. Howard – 2010

A Second Helping of Desserts: More Sweet Quilts Using Pre-cut Fabric
    by Edie McGinnis – 2010

Hot Off the Press Patterns

Cabin in the Stars by Jan Patek – 2009

Arts & Crafts Sunflower by Barbara Brackman – 2009

Birthday Cake by Barbara Brackman – 2009

Strawberry Thief by Barbara Brackman – 2009

French Wrens by Dawn Heese

Queen Bees Mysteries

Murders on Elderberry Road by Sally Goldenbaum – 2003

A Murder of Taste by Sally Goldenbaum – 2004

Murder on a Starry Night by Sally Goldenbaum – 2005

Dog-Gone Murder by Marnette Falley – 2008

DVD Projects

The Kansas City Stars: A Quilting Legacy – 2008